Juries:
Conscience of the Community

MARA TAUB

September 2014

Luiz —
¡ FELICIDADES!

maia

CHARDON PRESS
Berkeley, CA

Library of Congress Catalog Card Number: 98-73440
ISBN 1-890759-05-8

Cover design by Janice St. Marie, Santa Fe, NM
Cover illustration by Rini Templeton
Book design by Cici Kinsman, C² Graphics, Oakland, CA
Editing by Nancy Adess
Printed in the United States of America
Printed on recycled paper with soy ink.

Chardon Press
P.O. Box 11607
Berkeley, California 94712
(510) 704-8714
www.chardonpress.com

10 9 8 7 6 5 4 3 2 1

TO ALL OF THE DEFENDANTS

Contents

Acknowledgments viii

Preface ix

Introduction 1
READINGS
   Burden of Proof, by Catherine Crier 4
   Percentage of Cases that Have Jury Trial, by Jeffrey Abramson. 4
   Big Bucks and Criminal Justice, by Carl Rowan 7
   Teaching Prisoners a Lesson, by James Kunen 9

Part I. Imprisonment—Law & Reality

Chapter 1: Who Is In Prison? 13
READINGS
   Overview of Federal Prisons, FAMM-gram. 17
   "Arbeit Mach Frei": Racism and Bound,
      Concentrated Labor in U.S. Prisons, by Pem Davidson Buck 18
   The Million Mark, by Alexander Cockburn 20
   Thanks for a Nation of Finks, by Adam Langer 21
   Prisons Do Not Save Lives, by Robert Gangi. 23
   Unclogging the State Prisons, The New York Times 24
   Mandatory Minimums and the
      Sentencing Guidelines, FAMM-gram 25

Chapter 2: Undoing "Justice" 29
READING
   Convicting the Innocent, by James McCloskey 34

Chapter 3: Drug Policy and Reality 51

READINGS

The Drug Quagmire—Why We Should Withdraw from
Our Longest War, by Steven B. Duke & Albert C. Gross......... 56

Name Your Poison, by Craig Heacock 64

How Pot Has Grown, by Michael Pollan 65

Racism and the War on Drugs, by Clarence Lusane 71

Raids, and Complaints, Rise as New York
Uses Drug Tips, by Michael Cooper 75

Marijuana and Hashish, by Edward M. Brecher................. 79

Chapter 4: Who the Death Penalty Is For 84

READINGS

Death Rate Statistics, by NAACP Inc. Fund................... 86

Subject to Debate, by Katha Pollitt........................ 86

The Deadliest D.A., by Robert M. Morgenthau 87

A Modest Proposal for Executions, by Nat Hentoff 88

Sacrifice of Criminals as a Sacred Rite, by Hans Broeckman....... 91

Part II: What Juries Do

Chapter 5: The Value of Juries 94

READINGS

The Guarantees of a Jury Trial, from Duncan v. Louisiana......... 96

Life and Language in Court, by Robin Tolmach Lakoff 96

My Men and Women of the Year, by Alexander Cockburn........ 97

Jury Competence, by Valerie P. Hans & Neil Vidmar............. 99

The Strength of the Jury System,
from Huffman and Huffman v. U.S. 101

Two Major Changes, by Hans Zeisel 102

Chapter 6: How Juries Make Decisions 103

READINGS

Inside the Jury Room, by Valerie P. Hans & Neil Vidmar 108

Y'think the Jury System's Good? Read This, by Mike Royko...... 114

On Jury's Suggestion, School Renamed for
Black Official, by Associated Press......................... 116

Maria del Refugio ("Cuca") Gonzalez Vasquez,
by Debbie Nathan 117

Do You Swear that You Will Well and Truly Try?
by Barbara Holland 129

Jurors Go Against 3 Strikes, by Edward J. Boyer 130

Chapter 7: Jury Nullification 133

READINGS

Yellow Card, by Fully Informed Jury Association 135

Jury Nullification: The Top Secret
Constitutional Right, by James Joseph Duane 136

Juries and Higher Justice, by Jeffrey Abramson 141

Racially Based Jury Nullification:
Black Power in the Criminal Justice System?
by The Prisoners Self Help Legal Clinic 145

Chapter 8: How to Improve Juries 150

READINGS

A Jury System for Jurors, The New York Times 153

Power to the Jury: A Bill of Rights for Jurors, by Mary Timothy . . . 155

Juries on Trial, by Jeffrey Toobin 162

Conclusion 163

READINGS

The Need to Support, Monitor, and Discipline Police
by Rev. Virginia Mackey 166

The Judgment of Solomon, Christian Community Bible 167

Cowardice Asks the Question, by Dr. Martin Luther King, Jr. 168

Glossary 169

Resources 171

Index 174

Acknowledgments

✿   ✿   ✿

THANK YOU TO NADINE TAUB, my sister, who helped me so much with support and resources all along the way.

There are many people to whom I am indebted for many different kinds of help. Among them are: Andree Abecassis, Edith E. Adams, Nancy Adess, Cathy Ansheles, Grove Burnett, Judy Costlow, Carol L. Couch, Patricia A. D'Andrea, Clark de Schweinitz, Cindy Fresquez, Ida Friedland, George Gallegos, Pam Gogulski, Eda Gordon, Bob Gross, Luz Guerra, Naneen Karraker, Tracey Kimball, Elizabeth LaKind, Hillary Lamberton, Judy Levin, Alex A. Martinez, Judy Mayhon, Penny McMullen, Brian Mokler, Mary M. Mokler, Marie Nord, William R. Pabst, Bruce Rolstad, Jacqulyn Rolstad, Michelle Pacheco Skrupskis, Sarah M. Singleton, Bill Stanton, Haskell Taub, Luis Torres, Linda Velarde, and Mary Whiteside.

Preface

❧   ❧   ❧

As a juror, going into the federal building, up in the elevator and into the courtroom was like entering a self-contained, insulated world that was hardly connected to the world I lived and worked in. That formal atmosphere of dark wood paneling, where the windows didn't open, became symbolic to me of how separated the legal and judicial processes underway in the trial were from the people, lives and circumstances they would affect. I had to constantly remind myself that all the rules and procedures we were following had been developed, not by any higher power, but just by other human beings.

As a history and government major at a Quaker college and as a teacher since 1962, I had always considered juries important and wanted to be on one. When I received a short form to fill out from the federal district court in Albuquerque at the beginning of December, 1993, with a notice telling me to report for jury selection January 10, 1994, it seemed like a heaven-sent opportunity.

The trial was projected to be eight to ten weeks long; in fact, I missed the entire semester. The case, originally with 22 defendants, had nine by the time it got to trial. The defendants were accused of a variety of charges involving dealing in marijuana and attendant money-laundering activities.

On occasion, when the trial recessed early or the jury was excused for a few days, I was able to visit my classroom. My students, many of them marijuana smokers themselves, were interested in the course and outcome of the trial, which was covered regularly in the newspapers and on TV. It was clear they did not trust me—old, white-haired, Anglo and a nagging teacher—to do the right thing.

Their concern made me more thoughtful and anxious to understand the meaning of the situation, its implications and the bases for and justification of my opinions and later, votes.

As the trial continued, I became more and more convinced of the importance of considering its larger context—what the underlying issues were. Why, out of all those who had probably done things similar to what the accusations were, were these people being brought to trial? How could the jury maintain its independent judgment when it had no voice in deciding what information it would receive? How could the jury make a moral decision about the fate of the nine people at trial?

It was only after spending a day in the jury selection process that I realized that no one—neither judge, nor prosecutors, nor defense attorneys—had asked us to raise our hands, as they had so many times on other questions, to indicate if we had ever smoked marijuana. That seemed highly relevant to the possible condemning of marijuana suppliers.

As jurors, we were engaged in one of the few acts of direct citizen participation of our formal democracy. For our verdicts to be moral and responsible, they had to be put in a context and their consequences considered seriously.

Trial by jury was made part of our constitution by founders who saw it as a necessary protection of the people. Jurors are in a potentially powerful position; they have a unique responsibility to see and evaluate the larger picture.

"Fair and impartial" was the standard the judge kept using during jury selection. "Would that keep you from being fair and impartial?" Of course, what is seen as "fair" often depends on the experiences we have had, how we have been treated and on the information available to us.

How a jury votes is based on the interaction of a number of factors. These include, in addition to the actual conduct of the trial, the jurors' life experiences, beliefs and knowledge, which are used to evaluate the meaning and the worth of what goes on in the courtroom. That is why it is so important to have a true cross-section of the community on a jury.

This book, a collection of readings with introductory comments based on my own jury participation and related experiences, concerns the opportunity for responsible action that jury membership creates. It provides information that is otherwise difficult to find in one place about the actual workings of the police, legal and penal systems relevant to jurors. With more complete information, we can make better decisions in both our personal and our public lives. With better information we can also more effectively live out our most basic beliefs and work together for the common good. One way to do this is to serve on juries. I urge you to take advantage of opportunities to serve on juries and, once there, to examine and to vote your conscience.

Introduction

🌿   🌿   🌿

EACH TRIAL HAS ITS OWN COLLECTION of characteristics. In the Aguirre trial in which I was a juror, there were a total of 31 counts and nine defendants. It was a six-month-long trial with four months of courtroom presentation and two months of jury deliberations. It was in federal, not state, court and it was a criminal, not a civil case; no violence or victims were alleged. We started with four alternate jurors, not two, and were allowed to take notes. The jury was composed of 11 women and one man.

Half of the jurors lived in the Albuquerque area in the middle of the state and its most urban part. The remainder were from throughout the northern part of New Mexico. Northern New Mexico and Albuquerque are very different in history and culture from rural, border area southern New Mexico, where the defendants were from. No reason was ever given for the trial being held in Albuquerque.

Approximately half of us jurors were over 50. There were seven Hispanics, two Native Americans (Navajos) and three Anglos. Four were employed as mid-level "professionals," two as skilled workers, two in offices, two as waitresses and two were not employed outside the home.

Factors in Jury Decision Making

Many components, acknowledged and unacknowledged, go into juries' decision making. First of all, there is the totality of the trial itself,

1

its atmosphere and formality. This includes the setting: the building, the "security," the courtroom, and the deputy marshals. The marshals in this trial behaved like guards restraining us from doing anything wrong. They acted as though the defendants were guilty and deserved any punishment they got.

Second, the judge. Ours appeared also to have no doubt of the guilt of the defendants. He had a reputation for giving long prison sentences.

Third, the prosecutors. They sat at their table with "special agents" from several government agencies who had handled the investigation of the case. They never even looked at us jurors; they appeared supremely self-confident.

Fourth, the witnesses. The ones who testified for the longest period of time were the informant witnesses. Many of these, the slang for which is "snitches," had either been accused of or found guilty of dealing in a variety of drugs in much larger quantities than the defendants in this case were accused of. Some had originally been defendants in this case, until they had decided, or been pressured to "cut a deal." There were also witnesses who were the official custodians of various kinds of paper, such as motel, store, real estate, bank and government records. For the defense, there were character witnesses, as well as some of the defendants themselves. There were a total of more than 300 witnesses.

Fifth, the physical evidence. There were more than 4,000 pieces of physical evidence or "exhibits" in this trial. Most of them by far were introduced by the prosecution. The jury learned that any piece of paper with words on it, including utility bills and scraps of paper, could be referred to as a "document" and presented as an exhibit.

Sixth, the defendants. In this trial the defendants were all Hispanics, related to one family from southern New Mexico, near the border with Mexico. The six men were often dressed in blue jeans and cowboy boots, the three women in nondescript dresses and little make up. They ranged in age from their early twenties to late forties. They were neat, worried looking and as silent as the jury.

Seventh, the defense lawyers. Eight of the nine in this trial were "court appointed," because, although the defendants were accused of having made millions of dollars by virtue of their marijuana dealings and related activities, they had been found by the government to have a low enough income to qualify for court-appointed lawyers. The defense lawyers appeared alert and industrious. Including the two prosecution lawyers, there were a total of 11, all men.

Eighth, the potential penalties. An important factor in this case emerged during the cross-examination by the defense attorneys of the 25 or so informant witnesses: if the defendants were found guilty, the sentences were substantial—from at least ten years' imprisonment to life.

Also important in jury decision making is the jurors' opinion of the value or worth of both the laws and the penalties for breaking them that are at issue in a trial. In this case, the laws involved buying and selling marijuana and related money-laundering activities.

It bothered me that in the courtroom, "justice" always was equated with punishment.

The eight chapters in this book are divided into two main sections: Imprisonment—Law and Reality, and What Juries Do. Sources of the readings range from excerpts of court opinions to material from recent books on juries to newspaper and magazine articles and opinion pieces from both the mainstream and more specialized press. All the readings provide background information important for people to be aware of before being called for jury duty.

The following four short readings help to set the scene for later discussions.

❦ ❦ ❦

Burden of Proof

by Catherine Crier. From "A DOUBT based upon REASON as Raised by the EVIDENCE,"
USA Weekend, February 19, 1995.

IN MY DAYS AS A PROSECUTOR, we would begin jury selection by
asking prospective jurors, "How many of you came into this courtroom, saw the defendant and thought, 'I wonder what he did?'"
Many hands would go up. I would then point out that they had
assumed he's done something. This is improper. Unless the state
meets its burden of proof, the defendant must be presumed innocent. The government must prove the defendant guilty beyond a reasonable doubt as to each and every element of the indictment....

❦ ❦ ❦

Percentage of Cases that Have Jury Trial

by Jeffrey Abramson. From *We, the Jury* (BasicBooks,1994).

ALTHOUGH LARGE IN ABSOLUTE NUMBERS, jury trials constitute
only a small percentage of case dispositions annually. Relying on cen-
sus data from the 1940s, Kalven and Zeisel estimated that 15 percent
of all felony prosecutions reach a jury trial. A more recent estimate
is that less than 5 percent of state felony criminal cases are disposed
of through jury trial. In 1990, in federal courts, the 5,061 criminal
jury trials accounted for about 11.5 percent of the 44,295 criminal
cases terminated that year. On the civil side, jury trials accounted for
roughly 1 percent of the more than nine million civil claims disposed
of in state courts of general jurisdiction each year. In federal courts
in 1990, the 4,765 civil jury trials accounted for 2 percent of the
213,922 civil cases terminated over the preceding twelve months.

Numbers of Jurors Annually

Jury duty falls upon millions of Americans each year, making
the jury system the most widespread example of participatory

democracy in the United States today, despite all the loopholes that permit persons to escape service. As an example of state court jury utilization, Massachusetts summoned 905,795 potential jurors in 1988. Massachusetts courts use a "one day, one trial rule," where jurors who are not selected for trial during the first day of service are excused; those selected for a jury serve for one trial only. Of the number who received summonses, 314,343 were scheduled to appear for the first day of service; of these, 253,436 actually appeared. From this number, 47 percent (118,277) were actually sent to a courtroom, and 38,797 were impaneled.

In federal district courts, over 400,000 persons were present for voir dire in jury trials during 1990. From this number, the total selected for actual jury service was 115,877. The sum of individual days served by all federal trial jurors was 825,020.

Fees

Fees for petit jury service vary considerably from states in which nothing is paid for the first three to five days and up to $50 thereafter (for example, Colorado, Connecticut, and Massachusetts), to states where the fee depends on whether one is selected for a jury (for example, Arkansas, Indiana, Michigan, Nevada, and South Dakota), to states that pay a high of $30 from day one (for example, Hawaii, New Hampshire, and Wyoming). Federal courts pay a daily fee of $40.

Criminal Conviction Rate (Including Guilty Pleas)

Of all criminal defendants whose cases were terminated in federal courts in 1990, 83 percent were convicted. In absolute numbers, cases involving 56,519 defendants were disposed of in 1990 in U.S. district courts; 46,725 were convicted; 9,794 had their cases dismissed or were found not guilty at trial.

Guilty pleas or pleas of nolo contendere accounted for nearly 72 percent of all dispositions in federal courts. Of all convictions, 86.5 percent were through guilty pleas or pleas of nolo contendere.

The National Center for State Courts estimates that in 1988,

66 percent of all criminal filings in state courts were disposed of by a guilty plea. But states differ widely, with California reporting that guilty pleas were entered in 87.2 percent of all criminal cases and Pennsylvania reporting guilty pleas in only 46.7 percent of all criminal cases. In Massachusetts Superior Court, guilty pleas accounted for 64.1 of all dispositions in 1988.

Conviction Rate of Cases that Go to Trial

Combining data for both bench and jury trials from nine states in 1988, the National Center for State Courts found that about two-thirds of all defendants who went to trial in those states' general jurisdiction courts in 1988 were convicted. A study of felony cases tried in 1979 in thirteen local jurisdictions found that the conviction rate in eleven of the jurisdictions fell between 64 and 77 percent.

The conviction rate in federal courts is higher, with 80 percent of defendants going to trial in 1990 being found guilty.

Jury Conviction Rate Versus Bench Conviction Rate

In federal courts in 1990, the jury conviction rate surpassed the conviction rate in bench trials. Juries convicted 84 percent (5,210/6,181) of the defendants who came before them. By contrast, the conviction rate in trials before judges was 62.7 percent (1,063/1,693).

Recent aggregate data for jury versus bench conviction rates in state courts is not available. But after examining data through the 1970s for felony cases in six states, a large county in a seventh state, and the District of Columbia, the jury scholar James Levine found that juries in these jurisdictions convicted 74 percent of the time, while judges in bench trials convicted in 64 percent of cases. Another study of over 22,000 felony trials in 1978 found that juries convicted 72 percent of the time, and that judges deciding cases without juries convicted 58 percent of the time. These numbers about jury severity throw into question one of the core conclusions Kalven and Zeisel came to in their classic 1950s study of the American jury. By comparing jury verdicts in 3,576 cases with the presiding judge's report of what verdict the judge would have rendered in a bench trial, Kalven and Zeisel found that judges disagreed with juries in approximately 22 percent of cases. But the disagreement was massively one-way—judges reported that they would have convicted in 19 percent of the cases where juries acquitted but would have acquitted in only 3 percent of the cases where juries convicted. On balance, therefore, Kalven and Zeisel found a net jury leniency factor of 16 percent.

The more recent data comparing jury and bench conviction rates suggest that the common view of juries as more lenient than judges on defendants may no longer be true. However, it is difficult to know whether judges and juries are hearing the same kind of cases. It is possible that defendants with particularly strong legal defenses choose bench trials in disproportionate numbers.

🌿 🌿 🌿

Big Bucks and Criminal Justice

by Carl Rowan. *Liberal Opinion Week*, February 19, 1996.

WASHINGTON—Much of America was upset over the fact that O.J. Simpson was able to hire a "dream team" of lawyers and a squad of investigators and "expert witnesses" during his recent double murder trial. Some people thought he bought himself an acquittal.

But Simpson's use of his money was trifling compared with the way accused murderer John E. du Pont used his huge wealth to buy the friendship of local policemen, get the governing body of Olympic-style wrestling to approve his estate as a training facility, and get a gentlemanly arrest.

Simpson merely hired high-price defenders *after* he was accused of murder.

Du Pont used his money in ways that made everyone turn a blind eye to his violations of law, his threats with a machine gun and his crazily erratic behavior *before* he exploded into what police say was the murder of a former Olympic wrestling champion.

Du Pont had enough money to create a high-tech indoor shooting range in which he taught marksmanship to the policemen of Newtown Township, Pa. The cops made him an honorary member of the police force. Small wonder that du Pont was allowed to unlawfully assemble many weapons on his Newtown Square estate.

The local cops had been bought off. Du Pont was the golden gorilla who could do as he pleased—even after police got reports that he was behaving crazily, even threatening one wrestling trainee with a machine gun.

When du Pont complained that the kidnappers of Patty Hearst were out to get him, and that his house was haunted, and proclaimed himself to be the Dalai Lama, his police friends adopted the line of his relatives: "He wouldn't hurt anyone except himself!"

Rich men don't become public threats; just "eccentric." Menacing someone with a machine gun is dismissed as "bizarre behavior."

When du Pont holed up in his mansion after the murder of wrestler David Schultz, the local police did the smart thing: they waited him out and froze him out. Had he been a poor man with no political clout, the tear gas, bullets and even bombs probably would have flown hours after the killing.

Why did U.S.A. Wrestling, the Olympic governing group, sanction du Pont's estate as an official training center? Clearly because du Pont gave the group $400,000 a year, although the group's president, Larry Sciacchetano, denies being "bought."

U.S.A. Wrestling became blind and deaf last summer when du Pont banned two black wrestlers from his training complex. *USA Today* quotes Chris Campbell, the chairman of a U.S.A. Wrestling committee that heard complaints about the ban, as saying that du Pont "was afraid of death and black meant death. He didn't want anything black around."

So du Pont banished the black wrestlers, a black car, everything black, from his estate—an act so crazy that its looniness alone, aside from any racial and ethical implications, should have caused the Olympic group to act. But a du Pont gift of $400,000 is, well, $400,000—far from chicken feed for a group whose total annual budget is only $6 million.

I watched an incredible television performance on the "Today" show Tuesday by John du Pont's 12-years older brother, Henry, and Henry's wife, Martha. She insisted that the people to blame for the fatal shooting of Schultz were those on the estate who had refused to press criminal charges against John du Pont after he threatened them. She said they could have done what the family could not: get John committed to a mental facility.

But another thing about money. It is especially difficult to get a rich man committed to a prison for the mentally ill, so great are suspicions that the would-be committers are only out to get his money.

Then after a tragic murder, as in this case, it becomes difficult to punish a rich man beyond making him spend a few years in a mental hospital.

The power of money and the political influence it buys are so great that we will never have a single standard of criminal justice in America.

ッ ッ ッ

Teaching Prisoners a Lesson

by James Kunen. *The New Yorker,* July 10, 1995.

THE TERMINATION OF AID to inmates for higher education is just the latest expression of our society's ambivalence about what prisons are for. We lock people up to keep them away from us, to humiliate, degrade, and condemn them, and to deprive them of dignity, privacy, and autonomy. And we lock them up so they will come out changed for the better, ready to live and work in our communities. These conflicting goals have been at war throughout the history of the American penitentiary....

PART I

Imprisonment–
Law & Reality

ONE

Who Is In Prison?

For the prison system to warehouse human beings, prisoners must cease, in the minds of the public, to be human beings....The system works best when no one judge, prosecutor or even defense lawyer—can imagine his or her son, nephew or brother as the defendant.

—The Correctional & Osborne Associations Newsletter, October 1994

🌿　🌿　🌿

The Beginning for the Jury

JURY SELECTION WAS DONE in just one day: Monday, January 10, 1994, in criminal case no. 92-486JC, United States of America, Plaintiff vs. Gabriel Rodriguez-Aguirre et al., Defendants. We found out whether we had been selected by calling the court on Tuesday afternoon to hear a tape-recorded reading of the names of those chosen. It took two hours to get through to the number. We had less than a week to rearrange our lives for what we had been told would be an eight- to ten-week trial.

The trial started on Monday, January 18. January mornings are cold in Albuquerque, and coming into the courthouse meant walking through groups of homeless people who appeared to have spent the night outside and to have come into the heated federal building's outer lobby as soon as it was opened in the morning.

Walking past the homeless people made me think about our easy acceptance of how crime is usually defined. Near the end of the trial, a newspaper reported that it had cost about a million dollars so far. That is by no means the most expensive trial in the country, but it is still a significant amount in one of the poorest states. This was to be the longest federal district court trial to date in New Mexico.

Summary of Charges

The charges against the defendants were many, complicated and confusing. The multi-page indictment was read to us once, by the judge, on the first day of the trial. We did not have a copy to refer to during the trial. Neither the testimony of witnesses nor the evidence as presented turned out to correlate very clearly with specific counts of the indictment. During jury deliberations we spent more than half the time attempting to sort out the government's case. All the jury members agreed that the prosecution's case was disorganized and repetitious.

At the beginning of deliberations each juror received a copy of 69 pages of jury instructions, which included the charges against each defendant. There were nine defendants, 17 counts and a total of 31 charges against the different defendants. Every defendant was charged in Count II, the legal language of which was to "unlawfully, knowingly and intentionally combine, conspire, confederate, and agree together with one another and with other persons whose names are known and unknown to the Grand Jury to commit offenses against the United States…that is the unlawful, knowing and intentional distribution of more than 100 kilograms of marijuana."

Gabriel Rodriguez-Aguirre was named in 14 of the 17 counts. Known as "Gabe" or "Cuco," he was the person the prosecutors seemed the angriest at, and was always referred to as "the ringleader." He was the only one charged in Count I, "continuing criminal enterprise"; it was the one with the heaviest penalty.

Since several of the defendants had the same last name, and since many of the witnesses, as well as the prosecutors, often referred to the defendants by their first names, I have adopted that practice for clarity and simplicity.

Gabe had about a dozen brothers and sisters; a sister, Paula

Denogean and a brother, Eleno Aguirre, were also defendants in the case. Gabe's two children, Doloras Contreras and Michael Aguirre were also defendants. The other four defendants in the courtroom were: Gabe's brother-in-law, Ruben Renteria, Gabe's nephew-in-law David Morales, a young woman identified as a girlfriend of Gabe's, Sonia Gallegos, and Gabe's former employee Saul Tarango.

Gabe was the only defendant with more than three charges in addition to conspiracy. In the conspiracy count, a total of 22 people were named. Four of them appeared during the trial as witnesses for the prosecution, that is, "informant witnesses," the remaining nine were unaccounted for. Their absence was never explained at the trial.

Where is the "whole truth"?

As the parade of witnesses being sworn in got longer and longer, I became more and more aware of the phrase "the whole truth" in the witnesses' oath. One of the money-laundering counts, involving the E & J Lounge, illustrates how many different truths there are.

As the prosecution developed the scenario, over a period of two-and-a-half months or so, three defendants took turns going to a lawyer's office with cash payments for a total of $434,000. The names of these three defendants later appeared on various legal papers relating to the lounge, including the deed. There was testimony that Gabe's brother Eleno and then later one of his sons managed the bar. The situation seemed clear and straightforward.

But defense cross-examinations of witnesses and later the defense presentation revealed a number of additional circumstances. Although the previous owner of the lounge was facing bankruptcy, he was not even aware that the bar was being bought until the transaction was all but complete. According to the testimony of two women who worked for the lawyer and received the payments, one person made virtually all of them; he called himself David Morales. That person, who was really Daniel Maynes, was not in the courtroom in any capacity during the trial, nor was the lawyer to whose office the payments were brought.

Daniel Maynes led the office workers to assume he was David Morales, one of the defendants. (Maynes was, in fact, Morales' father-in-law, a brother-in-law of Gabe, Eleno, and Paula.) One of the women testifying to the defense's version of events admitted that she had left her job at the lawyer's office because the series of events around the payments for the lounge made her uncomfortable.

Soon everything that was said raised more questions than it answered, not only about what had actually gone on and why, but also about why the prosecutors developed the presentation of their case as they did.

The following articles discuss some tactics used by police and prosecutors in making arrests and filing charges. These contribute substantially to the ongoing growth of the prison population.

※ ※ ※

Overview of Federal Prisons

FAMM-gram, January–February 1995.

A COMPREHENSIVE "SNAPSHOT" of who is in federal prison today was provided by Kathleen Kawk, the director of the Bureau of Prisons (BOP), in her June 8th testimony before the House Subcommittee on the Judiciary. Highlights from her testimony follow:

- There are nearly 99,000 federal inmates, 90 percent of whom (88,000) are confined in 81 BOP-operated facilities. Another 9,800 inmates are confined in contract facilities.
- The BOP employs 27,000 total staff.
- 61 percent of federal inmates are confined for drug offenses.
- Of the rest, 10 percent of federal inmates are confined for robbery, 9 percent are serving time for firearms & explosive offenses.
- The average length of sentence for federal inmates is 9½ years.
- The average length of sentence for drug offenders is 6 years.
- The average age of the federal prison population is 37 years.
- 7 percent of federal inmates are women.
- 25 percent of federal inmates are non-U.S. citizens.
- Racially, 37 percent of federal inmates are black, 60 percent are white; ethnically, 26 percent are Hispanic.
- Between 1960 and 1980 the (federal) prison population remained relatively stable, varying between 20,000 and 30,000 inmates.
- Between 1984 and 1995, the federal prison population grew from 35,800 to 99,000.
- The (federal) inmate population is expected to approach 130,000 by the year 2000.
- Between 1984 and 1995, the number of inmates in prison for drug offenses grew from 30 percent to 61 percent, and the average drug sentence grew from 2 years to 6 years.

- The number of women in federal prison has more than tripled in the past 11 years, from 2,000 women inmates in 1984 to 6,497 in 1995.
- The BOP budget for fiscal year 1995 is $2.64 billion.
- The President requested a budget of $2.98 (billion) for fiscal year 1996.

🌿 🌿 🌿

"Arbeit Mach Frei:" Racism and Bound, Concentrated Labor in U.S. Prisons
by Pem Davidson Buck. *Urban Anthropology,* Volume 23(4), 1994.

ALTHOUGH BLACKS MAKE UP ABOUT 12% of the population, 44% of people arrested for possession and 57% for trafficking in 1991 were Black, a disproportion which has increased from 30% of all drug arrests in 1984. Furthermore, at least in some areas, sentences for Black drug "offenders" are twice as long as for Whites.

The racialization of prison populations resulting from the "Drug War" would make sense if, in fact, Blacks and Hispanics actually were more involved in drug use than are Whites. However, report after report shows this is not the case. According to the National Institute of Drug Abuse, 12% of drug users are Black, approximately the proportion of Blacks in the population. Since the laws do not invoke racial quotas, but affirmative action for imprisonment is obviously at work, it is necessary to look at formal and informal "Drug War" tactics which produce racial imbalance.

Despite being called a "Drug War," a title which implies that all drugs and all neighborhoods are targeted, in actuality it is crack cocaine and minority neighborhoods which are subjected to surveillance. It is thus hardly surprising that those arrested are disproportionately people of color. Simply focusing on crack, or even on cocaine, would not produce a racialized prison population: 69% of all cocaine and crack cocaine users are White and 66% have jobs. Racialization is justified by persistent media representations of crack abuse

as a ghetto disease, a contagion infecting "the nation." The vicious-
ness of the contagion is exaggerated, so that it comes to resemble
AIDS, a disease without a cure. In fact, only .5% of the population
uses crack; only 20% of cocaine users reach the point of experienc-
ing serious drug problems, and most of them, having reached that
point, cut back on their use; furthermore, only 7.5% of drug-related
homicides are caused by the effects of a drug, and in two-thirds of
those cases the drug involved was alcohol. These are hardly the epi-
demiological patterns of an incurable disease run rampant. That
crack as a drug, rather than as a valuable commodity, remains a serious problem for some individuals and some neighborhoods is probably related not so much to the drug itself as to the inadequate pro-
vision of medical services, just as is the revival of TB. The National
Institute of Drug Abuse reports that 90% of those seeking treatment
are turned away for lack of space, which is itself a reflection of the
"Drug War" priority on law enforcement and interdiction.

Racial disparities in criminalization have been produced not by
actual drug use patterns, but by the deployment of two major tactical thrusts. The first is the street sweep; the second is legal changes
making it easier to imprison alleged drug offenders and to keep them
in prison longer. Both these tactics, combined with racial differences in
sentencing and in various forms of early release, have resulted in a vastly
increased prison population that is also increasingly monochromatic.

The street sweep, which, in its violation of civil liberties, would
never be tolerated in White or middle-class neighborhoods, "has
become the most common anti-drug measure....[They] ensnare virtually everyone present in an area at the time. Typically, all those taken
into custody are 'put through the system'—that is, arrested, arraigned
and detained even when the police lack evidence."

At this point the justice system takes over, having been efficiently
provided with "offenders." Drug "offenders" are encouraged to plead
guilty, and "most,...including most of those professing innocence,
cop a plea to a lesser charge...." Such procedures, combined with the

street sweep which makes no attempt to discriminate between probable guilt and innocence, virtually guarantee that significant numbers of those in prison could never have been convicted in a trial.

Reprinted with permission of The Institute, Inc., from Pem Davidson Buck (1994),
"'Arbeit Macht Frei': Racism and Bound, Concentrated Labor in U.S. Prisons."
Urban Anthropology and Studies of Cultural Systems and World Economic Development 23(4): 331-372.

❧   ❧   ❧

The Million Mark

by Alexander Cockburn, from Throw the Bum Out, *The Nation*, November 26, 1994.

...THIS SUMMER WE PASSED, for the first time, the million mark for people in U.S. prisons (not counting city and county jails). Steve Whitman of the Committee to End the Marion Lockdown (P.O. Box 578172, Chicago, IL 60657-8172) calculates that the imprisonment rate for blacks is now 1,534 per 100,000, compared with a white rate of 197. The central aim of the crime bill, passed on August 25, is to lock up even more black people. In their book, *It's About Time*, the criminologists John Irwin and James Austin estimate that a set of laws akin to those just passed "would mean that most of the nation's 5.5 million black males age 18 to 39 would be incarcerated."

Check out the new laws on gangs and on cocaine. People designated as gang members can have their sentence for certain offenses (even those unconnected with gang membership) increased by up to ten years.

Of course, it sometimes amounts to a death sentence or a beating for a kid to refuse to join the neighborhood gang. "Affiliation" merely means the police put your name in a file. Mike Davis recently discovered that the cops in Compton had more names in their gang computer than there are male youths in the city.

The bill punishes persons convicted of crack offenses 100 times more severely than those convicted of powder cocaine offenses. There's no medical or scientific distinction between the two substances, but poor people use crack and rich people use powder. In

1992, 91.3 percent of those sentenced federally for crack offenses were black. Get five years for first-time possession of more than five grams of crack; get no jail time for possession of the same amount of coke powder....

❦ ❦ ❦

Thanks for a Nation of Finks

by Adam Langer, *Mother Jones,* May/June 1995.

Thanks for a nation of finks.
—William S. Burroughs

LAST YEAR, DON WAS A COLLEGE STUDENT in the Chicago suburbs, dealing marijuana and mushrooms to a small circle of friends. Bill, a college buddy, introduced him to Jack, who became Don's best client, providing much of the 600 bucks Don pulled in every month. But Don soon learned the truth: Jack was a cop and Bill a former dealer working for a narcotics squad in lieu of serving a drug term.

Don didn't serve any time; the cops signed him up. He set up two fellow students to expunge the drug charges from his record. "It's like conscription in the Civil War," says Don. "You can either serve the time or buy someone else to serve it for you."

Finks are big business. In 1994, the Drug Enforcement Agency shelled out $14 million to its stoolies; in fact, in 1993 alone, U.S. federal law enforcement agencies spent $97 million on all kinds of informers—four times what they spent in 1985. The percentage of federal drug cases where defendants' sentences were reduced due to "substantial assistance"—that is, finking—rose from 11.8 in 1990 to 30.7 in 1993. But some government officials are publicly questioning the use of finks, calling it "out of control" and a threat to the integrity of the criminal justice system.

Why squeal on your friends? It's a no-brainer: First-time, non-violent offenders face federally instituted minimum 5-year-without-parole sentences for possessing 1 gram of LSD, 5 grams of crack cocaine, or 100 marijuana plants with intent to distribute. A recent Cato Institute study found that drug offenders with no prior record are sentenced to one year longer in prison (on average) than violent offenders. According to a 1994 Federal Judicial Center report, 70 percent of the prison population's growth since 1985 is attributable to these lengthy drug sentences.

So finkers, fearing long stints in the joint, reach out and touch someone. Grateful Dead concerts are exceptionally fertile ground. Rob Lake, doing time in a prison in Jefferson City, Mo., was set up by a Deadhead after being approached at a concert. Louie Olmeda is serving 10 years in a Greencastle, Ind., prison for distributing LSD to another Deadhead, who set him up "in exchange for a lighter sentence and the return of his tour bus."

Groups against mandatory minimum sentencing lobbied successfully for a "safety valve" in President Clinton's crime bill that leaves imposing such sentences to a judge's discretion. But the new Congress' spin on the bill may ensure that finking will persist, except for the few dealers who maintain some semblance of honor.

Deadhead M. Reddick still has more than three years left on the sentence he is serving in Maxwell, Ala., because he wouldn't rat on anyone else. "I walk around here with my head held high, because nobody's in prison for what I said," says Reddick. "For that reason, I can do my sentence. No problem."

‼ ‼ ‼

Prisons Do Not Save Lives

by Robert Gangi, Executive Director, Correctional Association of NY.
Letter to the Editor, *The New York Times,* June 14, 1994.

A.M. ROSENTHAL'S JUNE 3RD column "Prisons Save Lives" is not the first time he has promoted the mistaken notion that building more prisons would be a good thing. In hopes of enlightening him once and for all, I would like to present an alternative set of facts and viewpoints that contradict his claims and conclusions.

Most people sent to prison are not violent, predatory criminals. Each year, for example, 60% of prison commitments in NYS are for non-violent offenses. Many believe that alternative punishments, including drug treatment, are the most effective and economical responses to these less-serious offenders.

Expanding our prison systems does not reduce crime. NYS's inmate population has grown from 12,500 in 1973 to over 65,000 today—with little impact on crime rates. In fact, many criminologists believe that prisons are criminogenic, producing (and releasing) well-trained, hardened criminals.

Prisons do not improve the quality of life. Instead they hasten the breakdown of communities and families by warehousing inmates far from home and returning them ill-equipped for a crime-free life. Moreover, the crowding and lack of ventilation and adequate health care endemic to today's prisons greatly contribute to the spread of AIDS/HIV and TB.

The prison expansion that has characterized the last two decades has destroyed, not saved lives. It has been the political folly and moral shame of our time. The experience and evidence available now is sufficient, so that a journalist as generally informed and intelligent as Mr. Rosenthal should understand that.

Reprinted with permission of the author.

❦ ❦ ❦

Unclogging the State Prisons

Editorial, *The New York Times,* January 1, 1995.

IN A BREAKTHROUGH for common sense, Governor George Pataki has persuaded Republican legislative leaders to consider changing at least some of the sentencing rules that have clogged New York State prisons with nonviolent drug addicts who might be better served by drug treatment and other cheaper alternatives to incarceration.

The changes will target the so-called second-felony-offender law passed in 1973, under which sentences rise sharply for anyone convicted of two felonies within 10 years. That law mandates stiff prison terms for hordes of young, low-level drug users and dealers who are caught twice.

The law is a big factor in the extravagant misuse of expensive prison resources to house an expanding population of nonviolent drug offenders. In 1982, 11 percent of the new commitments to state prison were for drug offenses and 63 percent for violent offenses like murder, manslaughter, rape, assault or robbery. By 1993 new commitments for drugs had rocketed to 44 percent while new inmates deemed violent had dropped to 35 percent. During this period, the number of state prison cells expanded from 23,000 to 65,000.

In his final year in office Governor Pataki's predecessor, Mario Cuomo, tried to persuade the Republican Senate to amend the second-felony law, only to be labeled "soft on crime." The fact that the Senate finally seems willing to consider similar changes for Mr. Pataki, a Republican, speaks well of their new majority leader, Joseph Bruno.

The precise details of Mr. Pataki's proposal remain sketchy. But he favors giving judges the option to sentence nonviolent second offenders like drug users and low-level street sellers to drug rehabilitation, community service, job training or house arrest using electronic monitors. The goal is to free cell space for violent felons who will no longer be eligible for work-release under an executive order signed by Mr. Pataki or who will serve longer time if his initiative to end parole for violent felons is approved.

It has been clear for years that locking up large numbers of non-violent drug offenders does not stop the drug trade. Governor Pataki deserves credit for pushing a potentially more humane and less expensive approach. Much now depends on whether he comes up with sufficient money to provide quality drug treatment and strengthen programs like intensive probation that hold offenders accountable.

Copyright 1995 by The New York Times Company. Reprinted by permission.

🌿　🌿　🌿

Mandatory Minimums and the Sentencing Guidelines

FAMM-gram, February–June 1995.

TO UNDERSTAND WHY FAMM IS FIGHTING for the repeal of mandatory minimum sentences but supports the sentencing guidelines, it's critical to understand the difference between the two sentencing systems. This is another attempt to help you understand that mandatory minimums and the sentencing guidelines are not the same thing, although many lawyers use the terms interchangeably (and incorrectly).

Think of them as two separate books, Book I and Book II. Book I was written by the members of Congress and in it are lists of all of the mandatory minimum sentencing laws that they passed in 1986, 1988, and 1990. The sentences in Book I apply almost exclusively to drug and gun offenders and they are commonly five and ten years in length.

Book II was written by the U.S. Sentencing Commission, a non-partisan commission of people appointed by Presidents Reagan and Bush. It is filled with lists of sentencing ranges for all crimes, i.e., robbery, extortion, murder, sexual assault, wire-fraud, drugs, and so on. Guideline sentencing ranges vary between months in prison and life in prison.

These two Books are what a judge must look at when s/he sentences someone convicted of a federal crime. The judge's first obligation is to look at Book I because it was created by Congress and is therefore more powerful than Book II. The judge looks at Book I to see if Congress has already established a mandatory sentence for that crime. If so, s/he must impose that mandatory minimum sentence as a starting point.

Then the judge looks at Book II to see if the sentencing guidelines require any additional time added to the sentence. Because the guideline sentences for drugs are so high, in many cases the guidelines will add additional time to the mandatory minimum sentence. Most drug offenders in federal prison who are serving more than ten years are probably serving a 10-year mandatory minimum sentence with a guideline sentence on top of it.

The easiest way to explain how mandatory minimums and the sentencing guidelines work together is to provide an example:

John Smith is convicted of a conspiracy to distribute 5 kilograms of cocaine. At sentencing, the judge must use each sentencing Book to determine John's sentence. First, the judge figures out what John's mandatory minimum sentence is for the amount of cocaine involved. To do so, the judge merely looks in Book I and sees that Congress has decided that anyone convicted of distributing 5 kilos of cocaine or more must serve at a "minimum" 10 years in prison.

Next the judge looks at Book II and sees that the Sentencing Commission has decided that anyone with 5 kilos is in the sentencing range of 151 to 188 months. The judge finds this range by looking at a Sentencing Commission manual that spells out what each sentencing range should be based on the amount of drugs involved. Each sentencing range is given a "guideline level" and in John's case, that guideline level is 34, which corresponds to 151 to 188 months. If John's lawyer can convince the judge that John is a minimal player, the judge can give John a four-point reduction in his guideline range, taking him to level 30, which has a sentencing range of 97 to 121 months.

If John's lawyer can convince the judge that John has accepted responsibility for his crime, John is eligible for another three-point reduction. However, he won't be able to benefit from the reduction because it would put him below the 10-year (120 month) mandatory sentence that Book I said he must serve for that amount of cocaine.

In other words, John cannot be dropped three more levels for acceptance of responsibility because it would put him at level 27 which has a sentencing range of 70 to 87 months. That range is below the mandatory minimum sentence of 120 months.

If there were no mandatory minimum sentences, and John was a squeaky clean guy in the conspiracy, the judge could lower John's sentence to level 27 and send him to prison for 70 months. This is not a light sentence, by any means, for a peripheral, first-time, nonviolent offender. But under a guideline system free from mandatory minimum sentences, judges would be more able to craft sentences that fit the culpability of the defendant.

The sentencing guidelines are by no means perfect, but they are able to be improved upon every year through the amendment process. In 1993, FAMM used that process to help change the LSD guidelines. The guidelines also offer a realistic alternative to mandatory minimum sentences because they are already in place, have the blessing of Congress, and attempt to ensure uniformity of sentencing in federal courts across the country.

Sentencing Guidelines Are Not Mandatory Minimums

Keep in mind that any changes the Sentencing Commission makes to the sentencing guidelines do not affect the mandatory minimum sentences. It is critical to understand the difference between the two sentencing systems and how they work (and don't work) together. FAMM opposes mandatory minimum sentencing but supports the sentencing guideline system. The guidelines are far from perfect, but they are a vast improvement over the rigid mandatory minimum sentences created by Congress.

It takes time and concentration to fully understand the difference between the mandatory minimum penalties (established by Congress) and the sentencing guidelines (established by the Sentencing Commission). Many inmates do not know if they are serving a mandatory minimum or a guideline sentence—or a combination of both. Many lawyers and judges use the words "mandatory minimum" and "guidelines" interchangeably, adding further confusion to understanding the two systems. But it is in your interest to learn the difference between the two systems because if any of the guideline amendments are made retroactive, and you don't know what kind of sentence you're serving, you won't know if you benefit.

The following examples show how a crack cocaine amendment would and would not affect a defendant's sentence: If Joe is a nonviolent first offender, convicted of possession with intent to distribute 200 grams of crack, he will automatically be given a 10-year mandatory minimum sentence because his offense involved 10 grams or more of crack (the required amount to trigger a 10-year mandatory minimum sentence). Under the current guideline system, Joe would also receive an additional 31 months, bringing his sentence to 151 months.

If the new guideline is approved, Joe would still be required to serve the 10 years under the mandatory minimum sentence, but there would be no additional time required under the sentencing guidelines. The reason for that is because the guideline sentencing chart would equate crack and powder cocaine at current levels of powder cocaine, and under the guidelines 200 grams of powder cocaine carries a sentence of 33 months. Therefore, the guidelines would not drive Joe's sentence higher than the mandatory minimum of 10 years.

An example of someone who would not benefit from the guideline change at all is Mike, a nonviolent first offender convicted of possessing 5 grams of crack cocaine. His sentence would still be 5 years, as required under the mandatory minimum penalty for possession of 5 grams of crack cocaine.

TWO

Undoing "Justice"

If anyone thinks there's fairness in the moral sense in the justice field, they're going to be disappointed.

—Bruce Kaufman, former New Mexico State District Court Judge.

🌿   🌿   🌿

THE FLAVOR OF THE PROCEEDINGS was as if the trial were some kind of sports event, very much a contest. The judge and the prosecutors and all the various other court officials were playing different positions on the same—the home—team. The defendants and their attorneys were the visiting team and the underdogs—no one was rooting for them. Somehow they had a reputation for playing dirty, at the very least, for being from the wrong side of the tracks.

The judge had not one person of color working for him—not a secretary, not a courtroom deputy, not a permanent law clerk, not a law clerk. In the hallway behind the courtroom, there were large photographs and brief descriptions of several other of the judge's big drug cases. These the government had "won"; large amounts of drugs and cash had been confiscated and a number of people had been sent to prison for a very long time.

We, the jurors, knew less than anybody about the case throughout the trial, and it appeared that pains were taken to keep it that way. We also knew very little about either the judicial process or courtroom procedure. We didn't know enough even to ask ourselves how much of the way things were set up was standard practice and how much was due to the particular judge presiding.

From time to time we were told how important we were, but our treatment did not reflect that. We were controlled, isolated and uninformed. Nothing in our treatment indicated trust in or respect for us.

Only lip service was paid to our physical comfort and convenience. The judge was concerned that we like the pastry left every morning in the jury room. But when we mentioned that we would like something healthier, it was explained to us very firmly by the courtroom deputy that the court had a contract with a bakery and that was what we would get. We were welcome to bring our own.

The judge also expressed concern over our comfort regarding the courtroom temperature. And he "let us out early" on Fridays, like a benevolent elementary school principal.

Early on, the judge acted like the host at some awkward office social event, once explaining to us, while we were waiting for a witness, who was portrayed in a courtroom painting. The atmosphere made it clear to us that we must not talk in the courtroom except to respond in chorus to the judge's daily, "Good morning, ladies and gentlemen."

Meanwhile, we were desperate for more direct substantive information about the meaning of what was going on in front of us in the courtroom and what we could expect to happen next, not filtered to us through the judge or his staff. Many jurors turned to the two deputy marshals assigned to guard us for information.

The marshals were both Anglo men, retired Albuquerque police officers, who made their opinions obvious through their jokes, their conversation and their behavior. They said that everybody in prison claimed their innocence, that defense lawyers' speeches bored them, that they were for the death penalty, that they longed for the good old days when police could carry eight-battery flashlights with which they hit people, and that police never made mistakes in who they arrested.

They made it clear that they—blue blazered, armed and wired for sound—were there to see that the formalities were observed. And that as far as they were concerned, the appropriate outcome was a foregone conclusion from the moment of the early morning arrests of the defendants, almost two years before. (Some number of jurors also appeared to believe from the beginning that the defendants must be guilty as charged.) In addition, one of the deputies had a crush on one of the women jurors; he was forever making suggestive remarks to and about her.

We had heard that the judge liked to call the jurors into his "chambers" after the verdict, answer any questions they might ask and play the tape of the phone conversation he had had with the President when he was appointed as a federal judge. And indeed, immediately after the trial, ten of the jurors went into the judge's office at his invitation. He was furious at the verdict. He said that the Mexican businessmen the defense had named as the source of legitimate money made by defendants were some of the biggest drug dealers in Mexico. He said he would have thrown the book at the women defendants.

The New Mexico Code of Judicial Conduct, 1995 Replacement, states: "A judge shall not commend or criticize jurors for their verdict other than in a court order or opinion in a proceeding...."There is no comparable federal mandate.

THERE ENDED UP BEING TWO Aguirre trials. The first Aguirre jury, which I was on, did not convict any of the nine defendants. On July 12, 1994, after two months of deliberations, we acquitted three and we "hung" on six. The three who were acquitted could not be tried again on the same charges. When there is a hung jury, it is up to the prosecution to decide whether or not to try the defendants again. They decided to do so in this case. So a second trial started with six defendants.

One of them, Paula, in her mid-forties, a sister of the alleged ringleader, got sick during the second trial. This resulted in her case being separated from the others, her accepting a plea bargain and being sentenced, separately, in June of 1995. At the second trial, there were then five defendants. The alleged ringleader Gabe, his alleged girlfriend Sonia, and his daughter Doloras, in her early twenties, were three of them. The other two were Gabe's younger brother Eleno and a nephew-in-law, David.

The prosecutors changed the original indictment in early August, 1994, to add cocaine charges to the original ones involving marijuana only. This is called a "superseding indictment." It was a major change in the case and benefited the prosecution enormously. Yet for those of us who are not lawyers, it is hard to understand how this can be done. One of the defense attorneys was quoted in a newspaper article as pointing out, "Anything they say they know now they knew before the last trial."

The second trial was in November and December, 1994. The Albuquerque-based judge who had presided at the first trial accepted the offer of a semi-retired federal judge from Midland, Texas, a first cousin of Lyndon Johnson's, to hear the case the second time. It was held in Roswell, New Mexico. Roswell is known for a famous UFO sighting and for being the location of the state military institute. It is in the southeastern part of New Mexico, called "little Texas." More people from that area serve time in state prisons than from any other part of the state, according to the annual reports of the New Mexico Department of Corrections. All five defendants were convicted at the second trial.

I went to the sentencing. It was held on Thursday, March 30, 1995, in the same Albuquerque courthouse as the first trial had been. It was a solemn occasion, like a funeral. Relatives of the defendants who I had not seen before were there—it was a gathering of a large, Hispanic, working class family from the border region of southern New Mexico. There were sisters, mothers, daughters and children; there were also husbands, brothers and sons. Very few other spectators. I was the only juror from either trial. Not even the regular reporter who had covered the case in the newspaper from the beginning was present. This was, after all, a year after the original trial, which had received so much attention in the Albuquerque papers.

It took the whole morning, as the defense attorneys made a number of motions to try to help their clients. The final result was three long sentences—for Gabe, for his brother Eleno and for his daughter Doloras, who had three children under ten years old. There were shorter sentences for the girlfriend Sonia and the nephew-in-law David. The judge ordered the defendants taken into custody immediately. The two women broke into sobs. The nephew-in-law called to them as he was led away: "Stop crying. Show them we're strong." I had seen defendants transformed into prisoners.

I have taught high school drop-outs, push-outs and fall-outs since 1973. Many of my students had had relatives in prison and had been held at the "detention center" (when under 18) or in jail, themselves. They were very much on my mind when I was called to jury duty and again after the sentencing. In 1978 I taught in a "demonstration project" for paint and glue sniffers. For the first time in my life, I was working with young teenagers who appeared to have no future. It was very sad. I said to myself that in ten years these students would either be dead or in prison. I remembered in particular a boy who was called "Popeye" by his friends.

In the fall of 1988, "Popeye," whom I had written to and visited when he was at the "Boys School" years before, was getting out of prison for the second time and needed a place to stay, as his family had given up on him. This was a kid I had baked a birthday cake for when he was 15. For the three months he lived in my spare room, I was constantly struck by both his physical appearance—in ten years he had aged thirty—and by how dysfunctional he was. He found going to the grocery store more than he could manage. I later read that statistics show that the longer you are in prison, the more likely you are to return. He did.

This reading describes in some detail a number of blatant mistakes made by the courts and penal system and the effects they have had.

Convicting the Innocent

by James McCloskey, *Criminal Justice Ethics*, Winter/Spring 1989.

ON MOST OCCASIONS when it has been discovered that the wrong person was convicted for another's crime, the local law enforcement community, if it has commented at all, has assured the public that such instances are indeed rare and isolated aberrations of a criminal justice system that bats nearly 1,000 percent in convicting the guilty and acquitting the innocent. And this view is shared, I think, not only by the vast majority of the public, but also by almost all of the professionals (lawyers and judges) whose work comes together to produce the results.

I realize that I am a voice crying in the wilderness, but I believe that the innocent are convicted far more frequently than the public cares to believe, and far more frequently than those who operate the system dare to believe. An innocent person in prison, in my view, is about as rare as a pigeon in the park. The primary purpose of this article is to delineate why and how I have come to believe that this phenomenon of the "convicted innocent" is so alarmingly widespread in the United States. Although no one has any real idea of what proportion it has reached, it is my perception that at least 10 percent of those convicted of serious and violent crimes are completely innocent. Those whose business it is to convict or to defend would more than likely concede to such mistakes occurring in only 1 percent of cases, if that. Regardless of where the reader places his estimate, these percentages, when converted into absolute numbers, tell us that thousands and even tens of thousands of innocent people languish in prisons across the nation.

Allow me to outline briefly the ground of experience on which I stand and speak. For the past eight years I have been working full time on behalf of the innocent in prison. To date, the nonprofit organization I founded to do this work has freed and vindicated three innocent lifers in New Jersey. Another, on Texas's death row, has been declared "innocent" by a specially appointed evidentiary hearing judge, who has recommended a new trial to Texas's highest court. Currently we are working on ten cases across the country (New Jersey, Pennsylvania, Virginia, Louisiana, Texas, and California). We have received well over 1000 requests for assistance and have developed extensive files on more than 500 of these requests, which come to us daily from every state of the nation from those who have been convicted, or from their advocates, proclaiming their innocence. We serve as active advisors on many of those cases.

Besides being innocent and serving life or death sentences, our beneficiaries have lost their legal appeals. Their freedom can be secured only by developing new evidence sufficient to earn a retrial. This new evidence must materially demonstrate either that the person is not guilty or that the key state witnesses lied in critical areas of their testimony. We are not lawyers. We are concerned only with whether the person is in fact completely not guilty in that he or she had nothing whatsoever to do with the crime. When we enter the case it is usually five to fifteen years after the conviction. Our sole focus is to reexamine the factual foundation of the conviction—to conduct an exhaustive investigation of the cast of characters and the circumstances in the case, however long that might take.

We find and interview as often as necessary anyone who has knowledge about the case and/or the people who are related to the case. We search for documentation and employ whatever forensic scientific tests are available that in any way shed light on, point to, or establish the truth of the matter. While developing this new information, we retain and work with the most suitable attorney in seeking judicial relief for our clients. We raise and disburse whatever funds are required to meet the legal, investigative, and administrative costs of seeking justice for these otherwise forgotten and forsaken souls buried in our prisons all across the land.

Appellate Relief for the Convicted Innocent

As all lawyers and jurists know, but most lay people do not, innocence or guilt is irrelevant when seeking redress in appellate courts. As the noted attorney F. Lee Bailey observed, "Appellate courts have only one function, and that is to correct legal mistakes of a serious nature made by a judge at a lower level. Should a jury have erred by believing a lying witness, or by drawing an attractive but misleading inference, there is nothing to appeal." So, if the imprisoned innocent person is unable to persuade the appellate judges of any legal errors at trial, and generally he cannot, even though he suffered the ultimate trial error, he has no recourse. Nothing can be done legally to free him unless new evidence somehow surfaces that impeaches the validity of the conviction. Commonly, the incarcerated innocent are rubber-stamped into oblivion throughout the appeals process, both at the state and at the federal level.

So where does that leave the innocent person once he is convicted? Dead in the water, that's where! He is screaming his head off that he is innocent, but no one believes him. One of our beneficiaries standing before his sentencing judge told him, "Your Honor ... I will eat a stone, I will eat dust, I will eat anything worse in the world for me to prove my innocence. I am not the man. I am innocent. I am not the man." The jury didn't believe him. The judge didn't. Certainly the prosecutor didn't, and more importantly than all of these put together, neither did his trial attorney nor his appellate lawyer. And so it goes for the convicted innocent. Their cries of innocence will forever fall on deaf ears and cynical minds.

Once he is convicted, no one in whose hands his life is placed (his lawyer and the appellate judges) either believes him or is concerned about his innocence or guilt. It is no longer an issue of relevance. The only question remaining that is important or material is whether he "legally" received a fair trial, not whether the trial yielded a result that was factually accurate. Appellate attorneys are not expected to, nor do they have the time, inclination, and resources, to initiate an investigation designed to unearth new evidence that goes to the question of a false conviction. Such an effort is simply beyond the scope of their thinking and beyond the realm of their professional responsibility. It is a rare attorney indeed who would dare go before any American appellate court and attempt to win a retrial for his client based on his innocence. That's like asking an actor in a Shakespearean tragedy to go on stage and pretend it's a comedy. It is simply not done.

Causes of Wrongful Conviction

But enough of this post-conviction appellate talk. That's putting the cart before the horse. Let's return to the trial and discuss those elements that commonly combine to convict the innocent. Let me state at the outset that each of these ingredients is systemic and not peculiar to one part of the country or one type of case. We see these elements as constant themes or patterns informing the cases that cross our desks. They are the seeds that sow wrongful convictions. After one has reflected on them individually and as a whole, it becomes readily apparent, I think, how easy it is and how real the potential is in every courthouse in America for wrongful convictions to take place.

a) Presumption of Guilt

The first factor I would like to consider is the "presumption-of-innocence" principle. Although we would all like to believe that a defendant is truly considered innocent by those who represent and judge him, this is just not so. Once accusations have matured through the system to the point at which the accused is actually brought to trial, is it not the tendency of human nature to suspect deep down or even believe that the defendant probably did it? Most people are inclined to believe that where there is smoke, there is fire. This applies to professional and lay people alike, albeit for different reasons perhaps.

The innate inclinations of the average American law-abiding

citizen whose jury experience is that person's first exposure to the criminal justice system is to think that law enforcement people have earnestly investigated the case and surely would not bring someone to trial unless they had bona fide evidence against the person. That is a strong barrier and a heavy burden for the defense to overcome. And how about judges and defense lawyers? These professionals, like members of any profession, have a natural tendency to become somewhat cynical and callous with time. After all, isn't it true that the great majority of the defendants who have paraded before them in the past have been guilty? Why should this case be any different? As far as defense attorneys are concerned, if they really believe in their clients' innocence, why is it that in so many instances they are quick to urge them to take a plea for a lesser sentence than they would get with a trial conviction? So, by the time a person is in the trial docket, the system (including the media) has already tarnished him with its multitude of prejudices, which, of course, would all be denied by those who entertain such prejudices.

b) Perjury by Police

Another reason for widespread perversions of justice is the pervasiveness of perjury. The recent District Attorney of Philadelphia once said, "In almost any factual hearing or trial, someone is committing perjury; and if we investigate all of those things, literally we would be doing nothing but prosecuting perjury cases." If he is guilty, the defendant and his supporters would lie to save his skin and keep him from going to prison. That is assumed and even expected by the jury and the judge. But what would surprise and even shock most jury members is the extent to which police officers lie on the stand to reinforce the prosecution and not jeopardize their own standing within their own particular law enforcement community. The words of one twenty-five-year veteran senior officer of a northern New Jersey police force still ring in my ears: "They (the defense) lie, so we (police) lie. I don't know one of my fellow officers who hasn't lied under oath." Not too long ago a prominent New York judge, when asked if perjury by police was a problem, responded, "Oh, sure, cops often lie on the stand."

c) False Witnesses for the Prosecution

What is more, not only do law officers frequently lie, but the primary witnesses for the prosecution often commit perjury for the state, and do so under the subtle guidance of the prosecutor. Inveterately, common criminals who are in deep trouble themselves with the same prosecutor's office or local police authority are employed as star state witnesses. In exchange for their false testimony, their own charges are dismissed, or they are given non-custodial or greatly reduced prison sentences. In other words a secret deal is struck whereby the witness is paid for his fabricated testimony with the most precious of all commodities—freedom!

Such witnesses are usually brought forward by the state to say either that the defendant confessed the crime to them or that they saw the defendant near the crime scene shortly before it happened, or they saw him flee the scene of the crime as it was occurring. If I have seen one, I have seen a hundred "jailhouse confessions" spring open the prison doors for the witness who will tell a jury on behalf of the state that the defendant confessed the crime to him while they shared the same cell or tier. When the state needs important help, it goes to its bullpen, the local county jail, and brings in one of the many ace relievers housed there to put out the fire. As several of these "jailhouse priests" have told me, "It's a matter of survival: either I go away or he (the defendant) goes away, and I'm not goin'." Jailhouse confessions are a total perversion of the truth-seeking process. Amazingly enough, they are a highly effective prosecutorial means to a conviction. Part and parcel of a jailhouse confession is the witness lying to the jury when he assures them that he expects nothing in return for his testimony, that he is willing to swallow whatever pill he must for his own crimes.

d) Prosecutorial Misconduct

The right decision by a jury depends largely on prosecutorial integrity and proper use of prosecutorial power. If law enforcement officers, in their zeal to win and convict, manipulate or intimidate witnesses into false testimony, or suppress evidence that impeaches the prosecution's own witnesses or even goes to the defendant's innocence, then the chances of an accurate jury verdict are greatly diminished. Sadly, we see this far too often. It is frightening how easily people respond to pressure or threats of trouble by the authorities of the law. Our insecurities and fears as well as our desires to please those who can punish us allow all of us to be far more malleable than we like to think.

Few of us have the inner strength we think we have to resist such overreaching by the law. This applies to mainline citizenry as well as to those living on the margins. However, the underclasses are particularly vulnerable and susceptible to police pressure because they are powerless; and both they and the police know it. A few examples will illustrate.

In 1981 three white high school janitors were threatened by the Texas Rangers into testifying that they had seen Clarence Brandley, their black custodial supervisor, walking into the restroom area of the high school where the victim had entered only minutes before she had disappeared. Brandley was convicted and sentenced to death based on the inferential testimony that since he was the last person seen near her, then he must have killed her. Eight years later Brandley was exonerated by the judge who conducted his evidentiary hearing when one of these janitors came forward and told how they had lied in implicating Brandley because of coercion by the investigating law officer.

On the eve of the Rene Santana trial in Newark, New Jersey, which was a year and a half after the crime, the prosecutors produced a surprise "eyewitness" who said he saw Mr. Santana flee the scene of the crime. A decade later that same witness visited Mr. Santana at New Jersey's Rahway State Prison and asked for his forgiveness after admitting to him that he had concocted the "eyewitness" testimony in response to intense pressure from the prosecutor's investigator. Since this "eyewitness" was from Trujillo's Dominican Republic police state, his innate fear of the police made him vulnerable to such police coercion.

Or how about the Wingo case in white, rural northwestern Louisiana? Wingo's common-law wife came forward on the eve of his execution and admitted that she had lied at his trial five years earlier because the deputy sheriff had threatened to put her in jail and forever separate her from her children unless she regurgitated at trial what he wanted her to say.

And in the Terry McCracken case in the suburbs of Philadelphia, a fellow high school student of the Caucasian McCracken testified that he saw McCracken flee the convenience store moments after a customer was shot to death during the course of a robbery. The teenager was induced to manufacture this false eyewitness account after three visits to the police station. Among the evidence that vindicates McCracken are the confessions by the real robber/killers.

So, you see, it not only can happen anywhere, it does happen everywhere; and it does happen to all different people, regardless of race and background.

Another common trait of wrongful convictions is the prosecutor's habit of suppressing or withholding evidence which he is obliged to provide to the defendant in the interests of justice and fairness. Clarence Darrow was right when he said, "A courtroom is not a place where truth and innocence inevitably triumph; it is only an arena where contending lawyers fight not for justice but to win." And so many times this hidden information is not only "favorable" to the defendant but it clears him. In Philadelphia's Miguel Rivera case the district attorney withheld the fact that two shopkeepers had seen the defendant outside their shop when the art museum murder was actually in progress. And in the Gordon Marsh case near Baltimore, Maryland, the state failed to tell the defendant that its main witness against him was in jail when she said she saw him running from the murder scene. One has to wonder what the primary objective of prosecutors is. Is it to convict, regardless of the factual truth, or is it to pursue justice?

The prosecution is the "house" in the criminal justice system's game of poker. The cards are his, and he deals them. He decides whom and what to charge for crimes, and if there will be a trial or whether a plea is acceptable. He dominates. Unfortunately, his power is virtually unchecked because he is practically immune from punishment for offenses, no matter how flagrant or miscreant. According to many state and federal courts, prosecutorial misbehavior occurs with "disturbing frequency." When the "house" cheats, the innocent lose. Lamentably, we see prosecutors throughout the nation continually violating the standards set for them by the U.S. Supreme Court in 1935 when it said that the prosecutor's

> interest in a criminal prosecution is not that it shall win a case, but that justice shall be done....He is in a peculiar and very definite sense the servant of the law, the twofold arm of which is that guilt shall not escape or innocence suffer....While he may strike hard blows, he is not at liberty to strike foul ones. It is as much his duty to refrain from improper methods calculated to produce a wrongful conviction as it is to use every legitimate means to bring about a just one.

It is human nature to resist any information that indicates that we have made a grievous mistake. This is particularly true of prosecutors when presented with new evidence that impeaches a conviction and goes to the innocence of a person convicted by their office at a prior time, whether it occurred four months or forty years before. Not only are they coldly unresponsive to such indications but they quickly act to suppress or stamp them out. New evidence usually comes in the form of a state witness who, plagued with a guilty conscience, admits that he lied at the trial; or from a person completely new to the case who comes forward with his exculpatory knowledge. Without exception, in my experience, the prosecutor's office will treat that person with total contempt in its usually successful attempt to force the person to retreat into silence. If that doesn't work, it will dismiss such testimony as somehow undeserving of any credibility and blithely ignore it. This prosecutorial impishness reminds me of a little boy holding his hands to his ears on hearing an unpleasant sound.

The Joyce Ann Brown case is a poignant illustration of this kind of prosecutorial posturing. One year after Joyce's 1980 conviction for being one of two black women who had robbed a Dallas, Texas furrier and killed one of the proprietors, the admitted shooter was captured and pleaded guilty while accepting a life sentence. She also told her attorney that the district attorney had convicted the wrong woman (Joyce Brown) as her partner in the crime. She had never known or even heard of that Joyce Brown. With the district attorney fighting her with all of his might, Joyce sits in prison to this day trying to win a retrial as we try to develop new evidence on her behalf.

e) Shoddy Police Work

The police work of investigating crimes, when done correctly and thoroughly, is indeed a noble profession. Law and order are essential to a cohesive and just society. Because police work is fraught with so many different kinds of pressures, it is rather easy for an investigation to go awry. The high volume of violent crime plagues every urban police department. Skilled detectives are few, and their caseloads are overwhelming. The "burnout" syndrome is a well-documented reality within police ranks. Interdepartmental politics and the bureaucracy stifle initiative and energy. The pressure to "solve" a case is intensely felt by the line detective and comes both from his superiors and the community and from his own ambitious need for recognition and advancement. If today's climate of "burn or bury" them puts more pressure on the detective to resolve, it also gives him more license to do so by whatever means.

Too often, as a result of the above factors, police officers take the easy way out. Once they come to suspect someone as the culprit, and this often occurs early within the investigation and is based on rather flimsy circumstantial information, then the investigation blindly focuses in on that adopted "target." Crucial pieces of evidence are overlooked and disregarded. Some witnesses are not interviewed who should be, while others are seduced or coerced into telling the police what they want to hear. Evidence or information that does not fit the suspect or the prevailing theory of the crime is dismissed as not material or is changed to implicate the suspect. Good old-fashioned legwork is replaced by expediency and shortcuts. Coercive confessions are extracted and solid leads are ignored.

Before too long, momentum has gathered, and the "project" now is to put it on the suspect. Any information that points to the suspect, no matter how spuriously secured, is somehow obtained; and anything that points away from him is ridiculed and twisted into nothingness. The task is made much easier if the suspect has a police record because he should be "taken off the streets" anyhow. That kind of person is not only a prime suspect but also a prime scapegoat. An example of this is Clarence Brandley, who was mentioned earlier. He was arrested in late August four days after the crime and on the weekend before school was to begin. The high school where the rape and murder took place was flooded with telephone calls by scared parents who refused to send their children to school until the murderer was caught. The arrest of Brandley calmed the community, and school started as scheduled. It was after Brandley's arrest that the investigation then spent five hundred hours building the case against him.

f) Incompetent Defense Counsel

The wrongly convicted invariably find themselves between the rock of police/prosecutorial misconduct and the hard place of an incompetent and irresponsible defense attorney. While the correct decision by a jury hinges on a fair prosecution, it also depends on dedicated and skilled defendant lawyering. And there is such a paucity of the latter. Not only are there very few highly competent defense lawyers, but there are very few criminal defense lawyers, period. They are rapidly becoming an extinct species.

The current Attorney General of New Jersey not too long ago told the New Jersey State Bar Association that finding quality private defense attorneys "may be the most crying need that we have." He also told this same assemblage that unless there is an adequate number of well-trained private defense lawyers, there will be little hope for justice. Of the 30,000 lawyers in New Jersey, the number of those doing primarily criminal defense work is only in the hundreds. At this same conference the First Assistant Attorney General pointed out that 85 percent of New Jersey's criminal cases are handled by the public defender system; and he wondered if there would be a private defense bar by the year 2000.

This means, of course, that 85 percent of those charged with a crime cannot afford an attorney, so they are forced to use the public defender system. As competent as New Jersey's full-time salaried public defenders generally are, their resources (budget and people) are vastly inadequate and are dwarfed by those of their adversaries (the local prosecutor's office). Moreover, they are so overwhelmed by the sheer volume of caseload that no defender can give quality attention to any one of his cases, let alone all of them. So, in response to this shortage, public defender cases are farmed out to "pooled" attorneys, who are paid a pittance relative to what they earn from other clients who retain them privately.

The experience of these pooled attorneys in criminal matters is often limited and scanty. In addition, they do not bring to their new-found indigent client the desired level of heart and enthusiasm for their cases. All of these conditions leave the defendant with an attorney somewhat lacking in will, effort, resources, and experience. Thus, the defendant goes to trial with two strikes against him.

What we have discovered as a common theme among those whose cases we have studied from all over the country is that their trial attorney, whether from the public domain or privately retained, undertakes his work with an appalling lack of assiduity. Communication with the defendant is almost nonexistent. When it does take place, it is carried on in a hurried, callous, and dismissive manner. Attempts at discovery are made perfunctorily. Prosecutors are not pressed for this material. Investigation is shallow and narrow, if conducted at all. Preparation meets minimal standards. And advocacy at trial is weak. Cross examination is superficial and tentative.

Physical evidence is left untested, and forensic experts are not called to rebut whatever scientific evidence the state introduces through its criminalists. I cannot help thinking of the Nate Walker case, where, at Nate's 1976 trial for rape and kidnapping, the doctor who examined the victim the night of her ordeal testified that he found semen in her vaginal cavity. Walker's privately retained attorney had no questions for the doctor when it came time for cross-examination, nor did he even ask anyone to test the vaginal semen for blood type. Twelve years later, that test was performed at our request, and Walker was exonerated and immediately freed.

This is not to say, however, that we have not encountered some outstanding examples of vigorous and thorough defense lawyering that left no stones unturned. What a rare but inspiring sight! We could not do our work without the critically important services of the extremely able and dedicated attorneys with whom we team up. If only the preponderance of attorneys would heed the admonition of Herbert Stern, a former U.S. Attorney and U.S. District Court judge in Newark, New Jersey, when he addressed a new crop of attorneys who had just been sworn in. He told them that they were free to choose their own clients. "But," he continued, "once that choice is made, once a representation is undertaken, then that responsibility is as sacred to us as the one assumed by a surgeon in the operating room. You must be as committed and as selfless as any surgeon." He further challenged them to "be an advocate. Represent your clients—all of them—fearlessly, diligently, unflinchingly.... Withhold no proper legal assistance from any client. And when you do that, you thereby preserve, protect, and defend the Constitution of the United States, just as you have this day sworn to."

g) Nature of Convicting Evidence

The unschooled public largely and erroneously believes that convictions are mostly obtained through the use of one form of tangible evidence or another. This naive impression is shaped by watching too many TV shows like "Perry Mason" or "Matlock." The reality is that in most criminal trials the verdict more often than not hinges on whose witnesses—the state's or defendant's—the jury chooses to believe. It boils down to a matter of credibility. There is no "smoking gun" scientific evidence that clearly points to the defendant. This puts an extremely heavy burden on the jury. It must somehow ferret out and piece together the truth from substantially inconsistent and contradictory testimony between and within each side. The jury is forced to make one subjective call after another in deciding whom to believe and what inferences to draw from conflicting statements.

For example, how can a jury accept a victim's positive identification at trial of the defendant as her assailant when she had previously described her attacker in physical terms that were very different from the actual physical characteristics of the defendant, or when the defense has presented documented information that precludes the defendant from being the assaulter? Several cases come to mind. Boy was convicted of robbing a convenience store in Georgia. The clerk initially told the police that since she was 5 feet 3 inches, was standing on a 3-inch platform, and had direct eye contact with the robber, he must have been about 5 feet 6 inches tall. Boy is 6 feet 5 inches tall. Four teenage girls identified Russell Burton as their rapist on a particular day in Arkansas. Burton introduced evidence that on that day his penis was badly blistered from an operation two days before for removal of a wart. And a Virginia woman was certain that Edward Honaker was her rapist even though her rapist had left semen within her, and Honaker had had a vasectomy well in advance of the assault.

Criminal prosecutions that primarily or exclusively depend on the victim's identification of the defendant as the perpetrator must be viewed with some skepticism unless solid corroborating evidence is also introduced. Traumatized by a crime as it occurs, the victim frequently is looking but not seeing. Victims are extremely vulnerable and can easily be led by the police, through unduly suggestive techniques, into identifying a particular person. The victim in Nate Walker's case, for example, was with her abductor/rapist for two and a half hours with ample opportunity to clearly view him. She told the jury without hesitation eighteen months later that "he's the man." Nate had an ironclad alibi. The jury struggled for several days but in the end came in with a guilty verdict. As mentioned earlier, he was scientifically vindicated twelve years later.

When juries are confronted with a choice between a victim's ringing declaration that "that's the man" and solid evidence that "it couldn't be him," they usually cast their lot with the victim. I suggest that this can be a very dangerous tendency and practice. And this is particularly so when identification crosses racial lines, that is, when a white victim says it was that black person. Future jurors should be aware that identifications can be very unreliable forms of evidence.

Another type of evidence that can be misleading and even confusing to jurors is that offered by laboratory scientists. Results of laboratory tests that are presented by the forensic scientists are not always what they appear to be, although they strongly influence jury decisions. A recent New York Times article pointed out that there is a "growing concern about the professionalism and impartiality of the laboratory scientists whose testimony in court can often mean conviction or acquittal." This article went on to say that the work of forensic technicians in police crime laboratories is plagued by uneven training and questionable objectivity.

We share this mounting concern because we see instance after instance where the prosecutor's crime laboratory experts cross the line from science to advocacy. They exaggerate the results of their analysis of hairs, fibers, blood, or semen in such a manner that it is absolutely devastating to the defendant. To put the defendants at a further disadvantage, the defense attorneys do not educate themselves in the forensic science in question, and therefore conduct a weak cross-examination. Also, in many cases, the defense does not call in its own forensic experts, whose testimony in numerous instances could severely damage the state's scientific analysis.

One case profoundly reflects this common cause of numerous unjust convictions. Roger Coleman sits on Virginia's death row today primarily because the Commonwealth's Bureau of Forensic Science expert testified that the two foreign pubic hairs found on the murdered victim were "consistent" with Mr. Coleman's, and that it was "unlikely" that these hairs came from someone other than Mr. Coleman. The defense offered nothing in rebuttal, so this testimony stood unchallenged. In a post-conviction hearing Mr. Coleman's new lawyer introduced the testimony of a forensic hair specialist who had twenty-five years of experience with the F.B.I. He testified that "it is improper to conclude that it is likely that hairs came from a particular person simply because they are consistent with that person's hair because hairs belonging to different people are often consistent with each other, especially pubic hairs."

Another problem that we continually observe within the realm of forensic evidence is the phenomenon of lost and untested physical evidence. Often, especially in cases up to the early 1980s, the specimens that have the potential to exclude the defendant have not been tested and eventually get misplaced. At best this is gross negligence on the part of both the police technician and the defense attorney in not ensuring that the tests be done.

Conclusion

We agree with a past president of the New Jersey Division of the Association of Trial Lawyers of America who said that "juries are strange creatures. Even after taking part in many, many trials, I still find them to be unpredictable. The jury system isn't perfect, but it does represent the best system to mete out justice. They're right in their decisions more often than not." Remember when I quoted a former District Attorney who said that "in almost any factual hearing or trial someone is committing perjury." So, a wide margin of error exists where earnest but all too fallible juries are only right "more often than not" and when trial testimony is so frequently and pervasively perjurious. My contention is that at least 10 percent of those convicted for serious, violent crimes are incorrectly convicted because some combination of the trial infirmities described in this article results in mistaken jury determinations.

Everyone will agree that the system is not perfect, but the real question is this: To what extent do its imperfections prevail? I contend that for all the reasons detailed above the system is a far leakier cistern than any among us has ever imagined. Untold numbers of innocents have tumbled into the dark pit of prison. Some of them have eventually gained their freedom, but a majority remain buried in prison, completely forsaken and forgotten by the outside world.

Other than my own wholly inadequate organization, no person or agency, private or public, exists anywhere that works full time and serves exclusively as an advocate and arm for the innocent in prison. The body of justice that has evolved over the centuries has many members. But not one part that functions within this whole has been created or is properly equipped specifically to secure the freedom of the incarcerated innocent.

Reprinted with permission of James C. McCloskey.

THREE

Drug Policy and Reality

African-Americans represent 12% of the U.S. population and 13% of monthly drug users; they account for 35% of arrests, 55% of convictions and 74% of all prison sentences for drug possession...

—The Sentencing Project, October 1995

🌿　🌿　🌿

IN THE AGUIRRE TRIAL, the government prosecutors always referred to the substance that the defendants were alleged to be buying and selling in large quantities and over great distances as "drugs." In fact, only one "drug" was named in the indictment and that "drug" was marijuana. The leading Albuquerque newspaper with the most trial coverage and statewide circulation adopted the prosecution's practice and also used the word "drugs" instead of "marijuana."

People who knew me and learned I was on this jury were always surprised at how much play the case was getting in the press and on TV when it involved only marijuana and money—no violence, no victims, nothing else.

One of the jurors, a nice and interesting person, mentioned in the jury room having smoked a lot of marijuana in the past and also having sold some. This juror was one of three who jumped back and forth from "guilty" to "not guilty" in voting on each of the 31 charges in the 17-count indictment—considering the evidence carefully in each individual situation. One day at lunch during jury deliberations, we sat next to each other. Since that juror had already mentioned having smoked and sold marijuana, I asked what the penalty should have been. The only answer was a shrug. The feeling I got was that if you're caught, you're caught and you pay the price.

This same juror also didn't believe how long the sentences were that the defendants would receive if found guilty. This was despite being shown jury members' notes from the trial concerning the testimony of the "informant witnesses" on that point. Several jurors shared the belief that the decision of "informant witnesses" to testify was not tied to any reduction in their own sentences.

Older friends of mine and my parents easily make a connection between the current legal status of marijuana and Prohibition. As children, we had been brought up on numerous variations of "bathtub gin" stories—and of the drinking that went on. An older friend talks about the good money—$25 a night—her brother made unloading ships for bootleggers.

Marijuana on Trial

In the case on which I was a juror, the prosecution alleged that vast amounts of marijuana had been bought and sold by the defendants. At different times, the numbers mentioned were 10,000 and 12,000 kilos and $30,800,000 (which the prosecution figured at $800 per pound to be 38,500 pounds or 17,500 kilos). Yet no marijuana was actually introduced as evidence by the prosecution in the more than 4,000 government exhibits. This surprised me. I was sure it meant something, if only that the government couldn't keep marijuana from disappearing with all the people who would have to handle it if it were introduced. I kept waiting for it to be marched in though.

There were a few photographs of marijuana and of packages alleged to be marijuana. The photos with the most marijuana in them were from what appeared to be another case, in Kansas, albeit one that involved some of the same people. Two loads of packages from vehicles were shown, one with cuts in them (like watermelon samples) that showed what was identified as marijuana. But the pictures didn't have any of the defendants in them, nor did they show the arresting officers.

I do not know the technicalities of "preserving a chain of evidence"; I do know we were supposed to be evaluating facts, but it seemed to me that the jurors had to take on faith that the people the government said were responsible for dealing with the marijuana were, in fact, responsible. A similar leap of faith was required to accept the prosecution's claim that the two large empty holes in the ground they showed pictures of were actually "storage vaults," prepared and used by the defendants to store marijuana.

Although enormous amounts of cash were said to be part of this case, only two worn $50 bills were introduced as evidence. One of the government's allegations, although not a count in the indictment, was that one of the defendants had buried at least $1.7 million in cash in his backyard, and then left a trail of bills to a gap in his fence. But it was unclear how much money had actually been buried or found, let alone who really buried it or why. Questioning by a defense lawyer revealed that there was an "internal investigation" going on to determine the full amount of money that had actually been found.

The government agents also said that they did not have the resources to count so much money and so it had been sent to Dallas, where there was a money-counting machine. The jury was shown a video of a money-counting machine counting money. There was no way I could tell whether the money it was counting was related to this case.

I did understand why the large number of horses (more than 200) whose purchase was said to be part of the money laundering activities in this case were not introduced in court, although I did keep hoping they'd be led in. There were not even pictures of most of the horses. The horses may have been one of the reasons the government prosecuted this case with such fervor. One horse, bought for $12,000 and on paper owned by one of the defendants, won the "All American Futurity" race on Labor Day weekend, 1991, in Ruidoso, New Mexico, at 12 to 1 odds. That race has the biggest purse in the country: $1 million. Many of the government agents involved in this case appeared to be involved in various aspects of horse racing.

The above may give some indication of why the jurors in this first Aguirre trial, although split on the verdicts, all agreed that the government's cases were loosely constructed and inconsistent.

MARIJUANA IS NOT MY DRUG of choice. But it certainly is for a majority of my teenage GED students, as well as for some number of friends and acquaintances. Many of my students say that they think marijuana is definitely better for you than alcohol is; that when they drink alcohol they get all crazy and fight and hurt each other and get hurt and sometimes get arrested. Marijuana, on the other hand, they say, gives you a buzz, but makes you mellow. It does not lead you to do things that get you in trouble, although you do sometimes get the munchies, or even become paranoid from it. Certainly judging from their use of marijuana and alcohol, I would say they are experts. As a teacher, I must add that trying to teach students high on either alcohol or marijuana is an exercise in futility, although it is the ones on alcohol who are aggressive and loud in their non-cooperation.

Street drug and legal drug use both affect health, although to different extents. Yet they can have very different social consequences. The approximately 500,000 deaths a year in this country from tobacco and alcohol use need to be paid attention to.

All the talk about marijuana at the trial made me curious to know more about its history and uses. I was amazed by what I found out. It made me feel such information should be more widely known.

A local printer who gives a discount to the small community newsletter I work on was interesting to talk to after the trial. He said that in his youth he had probably smoked enough marijuana to fill the room we were in. For the twenty years or so I have known him, he has been a fine printer, environmentally as well as socially concerned, experimenting with soy ink and supporting the local Tibetan refugee community. It was he who first told me that the Declaration of Independence was written on hemp paper; that is, paper made from marijuana stalk fiber. This is the kind of fact my students already know, but is new to me.

According to *Drugs, Crime and the Justice System: A National Report* (U.S. Department of Justice), marijuana was legal, at least in some places in the United States, until 1937.

Although I made a lot of phone calls to agencies in Washington D.C., I could discover no statistics reflecting the number of federal prisoners who are incarcerated because of marijuana-related convictions. These would include convictions for possession, distribution, trafficking, money laundering, conspiracy and continuing criminal enterprise. Statistics on all substances the government treats as street drugs are lumped together. They show that more than 60% of federal prisoners (and similar percentages of state prisoners) are incarcerated on "drug related" charges.

These five articles provide some historical background and analysis of both the social and personal costs of using marijuana and other street drugs. They also discuss the consequences of public policies regarding these drugs.

The Drug Quagmire—Why We Should Withdraw from America's Longest War

by Steven B. Duke and Albert C. Gross. From *America's Longest War: Rethinking Our Tragic Crusade Against Drugs* (Tarcher/Putnam, 1993).

The chief cause of problems is solutions.

—Eric Sevareid

THERE ARE TWO COMPONENTS of the "drug problem," both of which are "but for" causes of our dreadful drug disease. The first is the human appetite for drugs and the costs of feeding that appetite. This is the baseline drug problem that would exist in a free market where the government took a neutral stance on consumption of and commerce in drugs. The second component is the consequences of efforts to prevent commerce in drugs; the costs and casualties of the drug war itself. Neither component alone accounts for anything, because neither exists alone. But to understand the drug problem, we do need, analytically, to separate its two parts.

The Evils of Drug Consumption Per Se

Adverse Effects on Physical Health. The specific health effects of particular recreational drugs are often hotly debated scientific questions. Some of the recreational drugs, such as tobacco and alcohol, commonly cause major long-term illnesses or life-threatening acute health crises for habitual users. Prolonged tobacco use causes cancer and cardiovascular illness; alcohol abuse causes cirrhosis of the liver and other illnesses; and cocaine, if snorted, can cause damage to nostrils and nasal membranes. If smoked, cocaine may cause lung damage. However consumed, cocaine can occasionally kill its user. Marijuana, if smoked, might cause lung cancer, although that has not been established. Marijuana is often blamed for genetic damage and suppression of the immune response, but the evidence warranting these concerns is weak.

The risks of psychoactive drug use are substantial but no

greater than those accompanying many other recreational activities. The task for policy makers is to assess the relative risks of illegal drugs and compare those risks to others we take, or permit others to take, with hardly any qualms—hang-gliding, motorcycle riding, hunting, bicycle riding, boating, boxing, mountain climbing, and so forth. Policy makers should then decide what we are willing to pay for efforts to reduce or control the risks of taking drugs. The risks are not nearly as great as is commonly supposed, nor can they be eliminated by prohibition. (In fact, the risks are increased by prohibition.)

Criminogenics. Prohibitionists also claim that certain drugs directly cause the user to commit crimes. Our drug history is replete with fears and phobias on that subject. Cocaine, for example, was said to make African American men bulletproof and inordinately dangerous. Opium was said to make the Chinese users sex fiends, and marijuana made murderers and rapists of Hispanic Americans. The facts are more prosaic. There is no evidence that heroin or marijuana are at all criminogenic in this sense. If anyone ever "went crazy" on any of these substances and committed a violent crime, it has never been reliably recorded. Alcohol is another matter. There is evidence, albeit not as compelling as is popularly supposed, that alcohol contributes importantly to violent crimes such as murder, robbery, and rape. It is clearly a causal factor in reckless and negligent homicide, especially when automobiles are involved....About 12,000 people are killed every year because an automobile driver was intoxicated....

Abusers of psychoactive drugs, whether legal or illegal, are...an unhappy lot. Some are mentally ill. The abuse of drugs may be a symptom of their depression and hopelessness or of poorly managed self-medication.

The irresponsibility and apparent laziness of many drug abusers is due in some measure to the illegality of their drug use....The anti-motivational effects of illegal drug use are, in any event, greatly exaggerated. Many, perhaps most, parents of teenagers who use illegal drugs are unaware that their children use such drugs. This is also commonly the case in marriages where one spouse secretly uses drugs....

Effects on Quality of Life. When any substance is used excessively, the quality of life is diminished both for the users and those around them. No doubt many of the 10 million or so Americans classified as alcoholics would consider themselves better off if they did not drink to excess....But 90 percent or so of the consumers of alcohol, who are not obsessed with it and who could give it up if strongly motivated, believe that alcohol makes a positive contribution to their happiness and even the happiness of their friends and families....

Drugs that America regards as illicit provide equivalent pleasures to many and far greater pleasures to some, and this has been true for centuries, in most cultures. In fact, use of both opiates and cocaine was common among upright citizens in America and elsewhere in the latter half of the nineteenth century. Freud used cocaine and advocated it as a cure for fatigue, foggy thinking, and many other conditions. Several of our presidents, including perhaps even the abstemious Abraham Lincoln, also used cocaine. Ulysses S. Grant was apparently a user of both morphine and cocaine, as well as alcohol and tobacco....

When these drugs were legal and were as widely, if not more widely, used as they are today, few serious problems with their use were noted. Few users found such drugs to lower the quality of their lives....

In a free market system hardly anyone would be a drug abuser who does not already abuse at least one psychoactive drug. The negative contributions of marijuana would be far less than heroin, cocaine, or alcohol.

The Costs of Prohibition

Weighing against the evils of recreational drug consumption are a multitude of evils caused by efforts to prevent drug use. Our drug-war approach relies heavily on criminalizing both the sale and use of illicit drugs.

Global Evils. We now consider as a violator of American criminal law anyone who knowingly participates in any phase of the process whereby drugs are introduced into this country....

Our government has also become a kidnapper. Our drug agents have gone to South America, kidnapped suspected drug kingpins, and forcefully brought them to the United States for trial....

We engage in extensive and costly efforts to persuade foreign authorities to arrest and extradite their citizens who have violated our drug laws. Sometimes we succeed. We urge the governments of these countries to prosecute drug producers under their own laws and to eradicate crops, destroy labs, and otherwise to make it costly for drug producers or exporters to operate. These activities force the major drug producers to create their own armies and to terrorize the officials of their countries into permitting their continued operation. The governments in country after country in South and Central America are thus perpetually destabilized.

Drugs produced elsewhere for our markets have to clear our border. That is not difficult. Most authorities estimate that at least 90 percent of the illicit drugs destined for the United States are successfully smuggled into the country. But the smuggling process, involving high-tech boats and airplanes, sophisticated secretion of the drugs, and counterintelligence that often involves bribery of our officials, is also very costly. Once the drug actually crosses our border, its caretakers, consignees, and purchasers on this side of the border are at great risk of being caught, convicted, and imprisoned. As a result, the free market price of cocaine and heroin is increased between 70 and 140 times! Imported commodities that would cost in toto perhaps a hundred million dollars in a free market cost $60 to $100 billion under prohibition.

The money spent by Americans on imported drugs is hard for the smugglers to get out of the United States. Moreover, America is still a pretty good place in which to invest and a wonderful place in which to spend and enjoy wealth. Consequently, the drug importers try to keep a substantial portion of their funds in the United States. They need banks to cooperate, either to get the money out of this country or to convert it into usable forms if left here. Hence, the money launderers, who help smugglers disguise their funds as legitimate. Since money laundering is a crime, recruiting and maintaining money launderers is expensive. Getting the money out of the country without having it confiscated is also costly and often involves bribery. The entire process corrupts domestic and international financial systems.

To make the smuggling of drugs more costly and less attractive, we punish money launderers, but to the extent we are successful, we help to push the money out of our banks and out of our industries. The money is either stashed away or physically exported in trucks, planes, ships, and cars to other countries. We thus deprive ourselves of billions of dollars of potential investments.

Corruption Costs. What is the result of all this money flowing in illegal, clandestine channels among armies of criminals whose lives are under constant threats from within or without? Police, prosecutors, judges, legislators, lawyers, bail bondsmen, witnesses, jailers, are all under great corrupting influences, and many succumb. Our federal judges are among the least corruptible in the world; scandal rarely touches them. Yet U.S. District Judge Robert Collins was recently convicted of accepting bribes in a drug case, and U.S. District Judge Walter Nixon was convicted of perjury in a drug case investigation. The corruption during Prohibition may have been greater than it is now, but there are reasons to fear that we will eventually exceed that level if we continue on our present course....

Crippling Our Criminal Justice System. Our war on drugs undermines our criminal justice process. It diverts resources needed by police, prosecutors, and courts for dealing with other crime....

Treating illicit-drug distribution as tantamount to treason—the attitude embraced by the most ardent drug warriors—undermines the rule of law and the freedom of nonusers in myriad ways. Shortcuts and circumventions of the Constitution are overlooked in the name of drug-war necessity, and criminal convictions in drug cases are subjected to little scrutiny. Rights of individuals to privacy of their homes, effects, and persons are routinely subordinated to the interests of the government in carrying out the drug war.

Seduction of Our Children. The multibillion-dollar drug business seduces our young away from more mundane, longer-term efforts to achieve material and social success in an increasingly competitive economic system. Educational efforts are hampered by the presence of the dandies in fancy clothes and costly cars who are so conspicuous in America's lower-income neighborhoods....

Health Evils. Much of the damage to health inflicted by drugs is the result of criminalization. Drugs are taken by contaminated needles because unauthorized needles are illegal. Drugs are injected rather than taken some safer way because they are so costly and injection gives better "bang for the buck." The black market is unregulated, so consumers have no assurance that the drugs they buy have the purity represented, or even that they are drugs: sometimes they are poison, or they are cut with chemicals that are more harmful to health than the drugs for which they were surreptitiously substituted. One who is cheated in the drug business cannot resort to the legal system for redress, but must look to extra-legal systems.

Redistributing the Costs of the Drug Problem

What most of us think of as manifestations of the drug problem are really by-products of criminalization. While there would be no problem if there were no drugs, or if there were no appetite for drugs, neither would most of these problems exist if drugs were legal.

These enormous costs of criminalization might still be a bargain if, after a few years of intensive enforcement efforts, the illicit-drug problem were eliminated once and for all. If we can be certain of anything related to this subject, however, it is that no such happy ending is possible.

We may reduce the number of consumers of illicit drugs by our drug war, but it is unlikely that we can have any considerable impact on the hard-core users, the users we commonly refer to as "addicts." Hard-core addicts have little to lose by threats of forfeiture or imprisonment. They have already lost, or soon will lose, family, job, status, property (or never had them to begin with). The threat of punishment has a hollow ring. Since addicts—daily or at least weekly users—may consume 80 percent or more of our illegal heroin and cocaine, we may greatly reduce the numbers of occasional users without substantially diminishing the overall demand for the drugs....

Unless we relent, our intensive criminalization of drug commerce will be so stressful that our society will disintegrate from the strain, as it has already begun to do in our inner cities and as some areas did during alcohol prohibition. Gangs will kill for fun, as well as for drug turf. Our cities will seem like purgatory. Our suburbs will also be plagued with crime.

We will eventually retreat from an unwinnable war, just as we did in Vietnam. But in the drug war, as in Vietnam, the dead will be gone forever, and the wounded will remain so for a very long time. We should deescalate now, and, at least selectively and provisionally, legalize.

Clearly, however, government has a productive role to play in reducing drug abuse. The government has engaged in laudable efforts to persuade people to reduce their intake of alcohol and tobacco, and with considerable success. Therapeutic assistance to abusers of both legal and illegal drugs has also been too successful to justify its limited availability. All users or abusers of any psychoactive drug, whether tobacco, alcohol, heroin, cocaine, marijuana, or any other, who seek help to curb or discontinue their use should receive such help at public expense. (The savings in health costs and crime alone more than justify the expenditure. Compassion need not enter into the matter.) Hardly anyone could seemingly disagree, yet help is often denied even the chronic addict on hard drugs. Both education and treatment work, and if we devoted the resources we now spend on criminalization to education and treatment, our costs of drug use would be drastically diminished, whether or not drugs are legalized.

Under prohibition, the innocent suffer at every turn. The users of illegal drugs do not bear even a fraction of the economic and social costs of their drug use; the nonuser bears a large portion: in unsafe streets, overcrowded, expensive prisons, diluted law-enforcement resources, hospital emergency rooms filled beyond capacity, and inner cities becoming unlivable. In a system in which recreational drugs were legal, virtually all of these social costs would disappear overnight. We would still have some health problems associated with drugs. We would still have deaths by overdose, perhaps more than we have today, but we would have freed tens of billions of dollars to attack the problem of drug abuse in constructive ways, including treatment, education, and meaningful vocational opportunities to those involved in, or tempted by, drugs.

We would still have heroin and cocaine abusers, just as we have alcoholics and heavy smokers, who would pose serious social and medical challenges. But for the most part, under such a system, the drug abusers would pay the penalty for their abuse, and the penalty would be greater than it now is because the alternatives or choices available to them—which they would be giving up to be or remain an abuser—would be far more attractive than they are today.

Excerpted from *America's Longest War: Rethinking Our Tragic Crusade Against Drugs*, by Steven B. Duke and Albert C. Gross, (Tarcher/Putnam, 1993). Reprinted with permission.

❦   ❦   ❦

Name Your Poison

by Craig Heacock. Letter to the Editor, *The New Mexican,* May 9, 1995.

EVERY TIME I SEE ONE of these ludicrous "Drug-Free New Mexico" or "Drug-Free Workplace" proclamations, I have to wonder.

Are we talking about cigarettes and alcohol (which kill almost 500,000 people annually in the U.S.), or are we just limiting ourselves to the few drugs that our government has decided are dangerous?

As a teacher here in Santa Fe, I see the results of this hypocrisy daily. At the middle school level, students generally buy into the "this is your brain on drugs" propaganda, and they are very willing to parrot the "just say no" dogma.

However, as students reach the high school years and begin to question authority, they quickly realize that they have been lied to. Their friends who experiment with drugs generally do not die, rob banks, drop out of school, or fry their brains.

Instead, they often find that the effects of certain illegal drugs are far less troublesome than those of alcohol.

These students then begin to question everything they have been "taught" regarding drugs. They begin to mistrust the government and our legal system. If marijuana won't turn you into an idiot, they reason, then maybe cocaine isn't so bad after all. In this respect, marijuana is indeed a powerful "gateway" drug, as it forces its users to re-evaluate their media brainwashing and begin to think for themselves.

Our kids deserve an honest look at drugs and alcohol.

Reprinted with permission of the author.

🌿 🌿 🌿

How Pot Has Grown
by Michael Pollan. From *The New York Times Magazine*, February 19, 1995.

...IN LITTLE MORE THAN A DECADE, marijuana growing in America...evolved from a hobby of aging hippies into a burgeoning high-tech industry with earnings that are estimated at $32 billion a year. That makes it easily the nation's biggest cash crop. Unlike corn ($14 billion) or soybeans ($11 billion), however, modern marijuana farming depends less on soil and sunlight than technology, allowing it to thrive not only in the fields of the farm belt but in downtown apartments and lofts, in suburban basements and attics, even in closets.

Fewer than 20 years ago, virtually all the marijuana consumed in America was imported....Today, thanks in no small part to the...Federal war on drugs, which gave the domestic industry a leg up by protecting it from foreign imports and providing a spur to innovation—American marijuana cultivation has developed to the point where the potency, quality and consistency of the domestic product are considered as good as, if not better than, any in the world.

In an era of global competition, the rise of a made-in-America marijuana industry is one of the more striking—if perhaps least welcome—economic success stories of the 1980's and 90's. Domestic growers now dominate the high end of a market consisting of at least 12 million occasional users; on Wall Street, in Hollywood, on college campuses, consumers pay $300 to $500 an ounce for the re-engineered home-grown product, and even more for the "connoisseur" varieties....

Home Grown Grows Up
...In 1977, President Carter had endorsed decriminalization of marijuana and even the Drug Enforcement Administration was entertaining the idea; 10 states, including New York, had already taken that step....

Today, the penalty for the cultivation of a kilo—2.2 pounds—or more of marijuana in the state of Connecticut is a five-year mandatory minimum sentence....In Oklahoma, cultivating any amount of marijuana can result in a life sentence. And jail time is not the only penalty I would face were the police chief to find a couple of pot plants on my property today. Regardless of whether or not I was ultimately convicted of any crime, his department could seize my house and land and use the proceeds in any way it saw fit: a new cruiser, a pay raise, whatever.

This is America in the time of the drug war. A relatively little-known aspect of that war is that many Federal and state laws have been rewritten to erase the distinction between marijuana and hard drugs like heroin and cocaine, on the Reagan-era theory that the best approach to the drug problem is "zero tolerance." Today, the Federal penalties for possession of a hundred marijuana plants and a hundred grams of heroin are identical: a mandatory 5- to 40-year sentence, without chance of parole. An American convicted of murder can expect to spend, on average, less than nine years behind bars.

Many Americans, perhaps recalling the legal and cultural climate of the 70's, wrongly assume that marijuana has not been an important front in the drug war. Yet under the crime bill passed last summer, the cultivation of 60,000 marijuana plants is an offense punishable by death. Nowadays, marijuana is seldom grown on that scale; pot farming is by and large a cottage industry in which a thousand plants would be considered a big "grow." Even so, there are more than 30 people in the country serving life sentences for the crime of growing marijuana.

With so much more at stake, the techniques of growing marijuana, as well as the genetics of the marijuana plant itself, have been revolutionized in the last 10 to 15 years....

What is perhaps most striking about the recent history of marijuana horticulture is that almost every one of the advances...is a direct result of the opening of a new front in the United States drug war. Indeed, there probably would not be a significant domestic marijuana industry today if not for a large-scale program of unintentional Federal support.

Until the mid-70's, most of the marijuana consumed in this country was imported from Mexico. In 1975, United States authorities began working with the Mexican Government to spray Mexican marijuana fields with the herbicide paraquat, a widely publicized eradication program that ignited concerns about the safety of imported marijuana. At about the same time, the Coast Guard and the United States Border Patrol stepped up drug interdiction efforts along the nation's southern rim. Many observers believe that this crackdown encouraged smugglers to turn their attention from cannabis to cocaine, which is both more lucrative and easier to conceal. Meanwhile, with foreign supplies contracting and the Mexican product under a cloud, a large market for domestically grown marijuana soon opened up and a new industry, based principally in California and Hawaii, quickly emerged to supply it.

...Eager to expand the range of domestic production, growers began searching for a variety that might flourish and flower farther north, and by the second half of the decade, it had been found: Cannabis indica, a stout, frost-tolerant species that had been cultivated for centuries in Afghanistan by hashish producers.

...The great advantage of Cannabis indica was that it allowed growers in all 50 states to cultivate sinsemilla for the first time.

Initially, indicas were grown as purebreds. But enterprising growers soon discovered that by crossing the new variety with Cannabis sativa, it was possible to produce hybrids that combined the most desirable traits of both plants while playing down their worst....In a flurry of breeding work performed around 1980, most of it by amateurs working on the West Coast, the modern American marijuana plant—Cannabis, sativa x indica—was born.

Beginning in 1982, the D.E.A. launched an ambitious campaign to eradicate American marijuana farms. Yet despite vigorous enforcement throughout the 1980's, the share of the United States market that was home-grown actually doubled from 12 percent in 1984 to 25 percent in 1989, according to the D.E.A.'s own estimates. (The figure may be as high as 50 percent today.) At the same time, D.E.A. policies unintentionally encouraged growers to develop a more potent product. "Law enforcement makes large-scale production difficult," explains Mark A.R. Kleiman, a drug policy analyst who worked in the Reagan Justice Department. "So growers had to figure out a way to make a living with a smaller but better-quality crop." In time, the marijuana industry came to resemble a reverse image of the automobile industry: domestic growers captured the upscale segment of the market with their steadily improving boutique product while the street trade was left to cheap foreign imports.

The Reagan Administration's war on drugs had another unintended effect on the marijuana industry: "The Government pushed growers indoors," says Allen St. Pierre, assistant national director of the National Organization for the Reform of Marijuana Laws. "Before programs like CAMP"—the Campaign Against Marijuana Planting, which targeted outdoor growers in California from 1982 to 1985—"you almost never heard about indoor grass."

The move indoors sparked an intensive period of research and development, including selective breeding for potency, size and early harvest, and a raft of technological advances aimed at speeding photosynthesis by manipulating the growing environment. Gardeners also learned how to clone their best female plants, thereby removing the unpredictability inherent in growing from seed. All these developments coalesced around 1987 in the growing regimen known as the Sea of Green, in which dozens of tightly packed and genetically identical female plants are grown in tight quarters under carefully regulated artificial conditions.

The Indoor Drug War

Few recent trends in the marijuana industry can be fully understood without reference to an event known among growers as "Black

Thursday": Oct. 26, 1989. That was the day the Bush Administration officially began Green Merchant, the first organized offensive in the drug war to take direct aim at indoor marijuana growers—and not only growers but also the legitimate companies that supplied their equipment and the publications that supplied much of their know-how. Along with a new Federal law that for the first time imposed mandatory sentences based on the number, rather than weight, of plants seized (5 years for 100 plants, 10 years for 1,000), Green Merchant radically altered the rules by which indoor growers operate. Six years later, the industry is still adapting to the new environment.

...In the last week of October 1989, the D.E.A. raided hundreds of indoor growers and dozens of retail garden supply stores in 46 states, seizing equipment and customer lists. Virtually all the stores targeted by Green Merchant had advertised in *High Times* or *Sinsemilla Tips,* and the raids scared off enough advertisers to push *Sinsemilla Tips* out of business.

Using customer records seized from the grow stores, as well as 21,000 additional leads that the D.E.A. says it obtained from the United Parcel Service, law enforcement agencies undertook investigations of thousands of indoor growers, who soon discovered they weren't as safe in their homes as they'd assumed.

With the names and addresses of tens of thousands of suspects now in hand, law enforcement agencies developed a large appetite for indoor marijuana busts...Once established, a marijuana garden is much easier to find than any white-powder drug operation and arresting officers are far less likely to encounter resistance. Another powerful incentive is the asset forfeiture rules, which were liberalized during the drug war to allow agencies to keep the proceeds of whatever they seize. Since the crime of growing marijuana is by its very nature tied to a particular place—a house and a plot of land—seizing the assets of pot growers is particularly easy. All these factors help explain why, according to Norml, there were more arrests in 1994 for crimes involving marijuana than for all other illicit drugs combined.

Whatever the rationale, the war against marijuana is expensive—as much as $1.7 billion in criminal justice costs each year, by one estimate....Last month, Gov. George E. Pataki of New York, looking to slash government spending, proposed relaxing the state's mandatory minimum sentences for nonviolent drug offenders, some of whom may even be released. If they aren't already, marijuana growers should probably be voting Republican, since Republicans alone have the financial incentive, and the political cover, to reassess the costs and benefits of the drug war they started.

Like D.E.A. campaigns before it, Green Merchant failed to close down the marijuana industry, but it has altered the way it operates. One response to the post-Green Merchant environment was...to decentralize operations, keeping each grow room as small as possible—ideally, fewer than 100 plants....Even if one garden were raided, others would continue to generate cash for a defense. In the wake of Green Merchant, growers also began paying attention to such mundane things as "effluents"—especially odor and heat—and kilowatt hours, since judges will now issue warrants to search houses emitting unusual amounts of heat or consuming large amounts of electricity.

Into the Cybergarden

Perhaps the most important advances in marijuana cultivation involve computerization, which promises to revolutionize growing and vastly complicate the work of law enforcement agencies.... Sensors will monitor the five important environmental factors (light, water, humidity, carbon dioxide levels and temperature) and feed the information to a personal computer. Using solenoid switches, a so-called "smart interface" and a bit of customized programming, the computer can track and automatically adjust all these variables, either according to a preset program or to instructions typed in by the gardener. Add a modem and a remote-access program, and the grower can tend his garden from anywhere in the world.

...The computer could be programmed essentially to self-destruct as soon as it detected a security breach and alerted the gardener, rendering it worthless evidence....In the future, the D.E.A. may find the gardens but not the gardeners.

...The credit for this most dubious of achievements belonged not only to the gifted, obsessed gardener and his willing plants but to the obsessions of a Government as well.

ℳ ℳ ℳ

Racism and the War on Drugs

by Clarence Lusane. From *Pipe Dream Blues: Racism and the War on Drugs* (South End Press, 1991).

Linking Drugs and Racism

...Drug trafficking and abuse has crossed all class, race, gender, and national boundaries and is a society-wide and global problem. But this is a problem with a distinct racial edge. What is cast as a "problem" in the White community is, in fact, a *crisis* in communities of color. The survival and healthy development of a whole generation of Black youth and community is at stake. A pivotal step in grasping the breadth and depth of the problem, and solutions to it, is understanding illegal and legal drugs in the African American community within a specific historic context....

Racism and the Drug Crisis

The war against marijuana after World War I also became a vehicle for attacks on the Black community. Although marijuana had existed in the United States for centuries, it wasn't used primarily as an intoxicant until the early part of this century. One of the first recorded incidents of marijuana smoking occurred in the famous Storyville section of New Orleans, which became a major marijuana importation and distribution center. Most of the marijuana came from Mexico, Cuba, the Caribbean, or Texas. From Louisiana, it traveled across the country to other major cities.

Many of the Black, White, and Mexican dock workers became smokers as shiploads of the weed came into New Orleans. As they moved on, they took as much marijuana as they could carry with them and helped to spread its use across the nation....

By the mid-1920s, however, a full-scale anti-marijuana campaign was in full swing. In 1925, Louisiana made marijuana possession and use a felony. Many other southern and southwestern states soon followed suit. Blacks and Mexicans became the main targets of this new wave of anti-drug fever....

Hysterical newspaper headlines and radio broadcasts blamed marijuana-intoxicated Blacks and Mexicans for many heinous crimes they claimed were being committed against Whites. According to these stories, similar to earlier ones about cocaine, marijuana gave Blacks superhuman strength and extraordinary and violent sexual desires....

The Hearst newspaper empire was the chief vehicle for the spread of these racial tales. It was the Hearst papers that first popularized the term "marijuana." Few realized until it was too late that the evil marijuana cigarette being attacked in the Hearst papers and by federal authorities was the same hemp plant that had provided so many useful and essential products for decades.

William Randolph Hearst's antagonism toward Mexicans and Blacks was rooted in both his own racist world outlook and in the service of his own greed. He was more than a little upset when Pancho Villa's army seized about 800,000 acres of his land during the Mexican revolution.

Also, hemp's use as a high-quality paper substitute threatened the lumber and newspaper industries controlled by Hearst, especially after the invention of state-of-the-art, affordable hemp stripping machines in the 1930s. The USDA was predicting that hemp would be the number-one crop in America, and even as late as 1938, one year after marijuana was outlawed, *Popular Mechanics* referred to hemp as the $1 billion crop. Hearst, along with the Dupont chemical companies, which had just invented a wood pulp process of their own, formed an alliance to outlaw hemp.

This federal side of this campaign was orchestrated by Harry Jacob Anslinger, who had made his reputation as a hardline law enforcer during prohibition. In 1930, he became director of the Federal Bureau of Narcotics and remained so for the next thirty-two years. Anslinger's agents helped to spread the rumors and tales about the dangers of Black and Mexican drug use. Success came for Anslinger in the Fall of 1937 when the Marijuana Tax Act, which made use and sale of marijuana a felony, became law.

Anslinger's hatred of people of color was legendary....In the 1940s, he ordered files to be kept on all jazz and swing musicians....

Anslinger became friends with right-wing Wisconsin Senator Joseph McCarthy and participated in the anti-communist witch hunts of the 1950s. Their fierce and frenzied battle against drugs and communists was the height of disingenuousness. Anslinger admits in his autobiography that he had supplied McCarthy with morphine for many years. His ludicrous and hypocritical justification was that he was protecting the junkie senator from communist blackmailers who could exploit his addiction....

Legalization and Decriminalization

Those who argue for the purity of individual rights, including libertarians and many progressives, believe that everyone should have the right to buy the drug of their choice without government interference other than for health regulation. Inherent in this argument is the assumption of social equalities that do not exist. The consequences of drug abuse do not befall groups of people regardless of race, and neither does the capacity to make informed choices about the safety and use of different drugs.

Legalization of some drugs, by all indications, would resolve some of the biggest problems of the current drug crisis and drug war. The violence and homicides associated with drug prohibition would virtually disappear. So would much of the arrest and incarceration of tens of thousands of people who are sent to jail on simple possession charges....

Legalization of drugs alone, however, would leave untouched the issues that give rise to drug abuse and their destructive impact on poor and minority communities. Issues of economic development, employment opportunities, access to medical services for addiction, as well as the despair brought on by homelessness and poverty are not addressed by the legalization option. In addition, the marketing of drugs to the poor and to people of color would, unless severely restricted, likely increase. There is no indication that substance abuse in these communities would diminish particularly, since drug use goes up with decreased productivity, increased social violence, or increased property loss. Once those issues are resolved, it's doubtful that the media or various levels of government will be pressured to make the drug problem a priority.

Perhaps the real question concerning legalization and decriminalization is whether a particular drug, legal or illegal, can be used responsibly. For those drugs—such as alcohol—for which it is determined that the majority of people in society can use [them] responsibly, legalization is a prudent and rational step if strict regulation and education and treatment services are available and accessible. In this context, the decriminalization for use and possession of small amounts of marijuana seems not only logical, but an essential step in mitigating the harm of the drug war....

Marijuana smoking does present some obvious health risks, such as lung damage for long-term, heavy users. Marijuana has a very low acute toxicity and is virtually impossible to overdose on. In the short term, the dangers of marijuana are similar to those of any drug or intoxicant that impairs one's senses, i.e., accident potential due to impaired memory, problems concentrating, and problems with limited peripheral vision. Furthermore, marijuana has been decriminalized in some parts of the United States....

For those drugs that are harmful and deadly, such as crack cocaine and ice, their use should be treated as a priority health issue and attacked in the way that the American Cancer Society has addressed the problem of tobacco addiction....

No policy options should lose sight of the fundamental goal of drug reform: community stability, just development, and the good health of individuals and society. This must be primary in considering the legalization of any specific drug as a tactical option. As long as economic and racial inequities exist, abuse will continue whether drugs are legal or illegal....

Reprinted by permission.

🔥 🔥 🔥

Raids, and Complaints, Rise as New York Uses Drug Tips

by Michael Cooper, *The New York Times,* May 27, 1998.

...AS MAYOR RUDOLPH GIULIANI'S administration has stepped up its anti-drug initiatives, forcing many low-level dealers off the sidewalks and into apartments, the Police Department has doubled the number of narcotics search warrants it executes each year, to 2,977 last year from 1,447 in 1994. Most of these are no-knock warrants, which authorize the police to break down doors without warning. The police say that a vast majority of raids yield drugs. But in a number of recent cases, the police have broken down doors and searched homes only to find terrified, confused families.

In at least a half-dozen cases in the last year alone, people who say that the police wrongly raided their homes have filed or announced plans to file multimillion-dollar lawsuits against the city. In each case, the search warrants were based largely, if not solely, on the word of confidential informers, who are criminals seeking to trade what they know for reduced charges, shorter sentences or cash.

Confidential informers—called snitches and rats by the narcotics officers who depend on them—are a central, if little-discussed, weapon in the war on drugs. Since the apartments many drug dealers now use are difficult and dangerous for undercover officers to infiltrate, investigators have come to rely more and more on their underworld contacts.

There have been several cases across the country in which drug raids based on tips from confidential informers have gone awry, sometimes with tragic consequences. In Boston, a 75-year-old retired minister died of a heart attack in 1994 after the police raided his home and handcuffed him, working on a bad tip from an informer. Another bad tip led drug agents to raid a house in San Diego in 1992. Its owner, a businessman, thought he was being robbed and fired a shot at the raid team. They returned fire, seriously wounding him. He sued and won a $2.75 million settlement.

Interviews with police officials, prosecutors, judges and lawyers paint a picture of a system in which police officers feel pressured to conduct more raids, tips from confidential informers are increasingly difficult to verify and judges spend less time examining the increasing number of applications for search warrants before signing them.

Police officials defend the system, saying their aggressive assault against drugs is one reason for New York City's historic drop in crime. While the Police Department would not release specific figures, Commissioner Howard Safir has said repeatedly that a vast majority of search warrants yield contraband and that the Police Department does as much as other police forces—if not more—to winnow out bad tips. He said that when a drug search comes up empty, it often means that the dealers have simply moved on.

Civil libertarians say it may be time to rethink a policy in which the word of a single criminal, who is often paid for his information, can be enough to send armed police officers to break down doors and invade the homes of innocent people. They note that the questionable raids have all been in the homes of black and Hispanic families.

The U.S. Supreme Court has upheld the use of confidential informers to obtain search warrants, and has held that "no-knock" warrants can be used when the officers fear that announcing their presence could endanger their lives or give criminals time to destroy the evidence they are seeking. But critics argue that the practice violates the spirit if not the letter of the Fourth Amendment, which protects against unreasonable searches and seizures.

"If the Fourth Amendment is about anything, it's about a distrust of this kind of police behavior," said Tracey Maclin, a law professor at Boston University who has written briefs for the Supreme Court on behalf of the American Civil Liberties Union in several cases dealing with no-knock police raids.

Judge Stephen Trott, who sits on the 9th U.S. Circuit Court of Appeals, based in San Francisco, and lectures widely on the use of informers, said they are inherently risky. "Confidential informants are like nuclear material, which, correctly used, can heal cancer but wrongly used can cause cancer," he said. "You need them to make cases, but by definition they are criminals, they are sociopaths, and they will lie about anything. That's why you have to corroborate what they say."

...Officials say that corroborating tips from confidential informers is often impossible because drug dealers have become more savvy and cautious. Investigators, they said, are being forced to choose between acting on a tip that might be bad or doing nothing at all.

"In the old days, a lot of times you'd have an informant and the observation of cops of the trafficking," said a Manhattan prosecutor who spoke on the condition of anonymity. "It's very difficult now to do that, because of the increased security measures taken by the dealers."...

Judge John P. Walsh, who supervises arraignments in Manhattan Criminal Court and often handles search warrant applications, said there is a two-pronged test for a warrant to raid an apartment based on an informer's tip. The application must tell why an informer is considered reliable—he has been used with good results in the past, for example—and it must show the basis of the informer's knowledge, usually a statement that the informer has been inside the apartment in question. First-time informers are brought to court and can be questioned under oath by judges.

But Judge Walsh said the increasing number of warrants had forced many judges to spend less time examining applications. "If you are getting one every two weeks, you can put a little more time into it," he said. "When it's one a day, you have to move a bit faster"—about 5 to 10 minutes per application, he said.

The Police Department refuses to disclose how many confidential informers it uses or how much it pays them for tips. Marilyn Mode, the Deputy Commissioner for Public Information, said disclosing such information would put informers in danger. Asked how, she said only, "Because it would."

One narcotics supervisor who spoke on the condition of anonymity described a sliding scale of payoffs. As a rule of thumb, the supervisor said, the police will not let an informer off with no jail time unless his tip brings in other criminals who would get five times as much jail time. Payments range from $20 for introducing undercover officers to dealers, to $50 for buying drugs to help the police build a case, to $500 for each kilogram of cocaine or heroin confiscated, he said.

In recent years, he said, the Police Department has vastly increased its roster of confidential informers. He credits a new policy that has the police debrief every person they arrest. One of the first questions they ask is: "Do you know anything about any other crimes?"

Those who indicate a willingness to deal are checked out and registered with the Police Department's Intelligence Division. First-time informers are tightly controlled. Some are practically deputized by narcotics investigators, who give them marked money and send them into buildings to buy drugs. The informers are frisked before they go in, to make sure they have no drugs, and frisked again when they leave, to make sure they have spent the money. This is called a controlled buy.

But once an informer has proven reliable, there are less stringent controls. The narcotics supervisor said that because the police have been under pressure to conduct more drug raids, he worried that young officers might be too trusting of informers. "There's pressure to get the numbers up," he said.

🌿 🌿 🌿

Marijuana and Hashish
by Edward M. Brecher. From *Licit and Illicit Drugs* (Consumers Union, 1972).

THE "WEED" THAT IN THE UNITED STATES and Mexico is commonly called marijuana, hemp, or cannabis is in fact a highly useful plant cultivated throughout recorded history and perhaps much earlier as well. There is only one species—its scientific name is *Cannabis sativa*—which yields both a potent drug and a strong fiber long used in the manufacture of fine linen as well as canvas and rope....

Marijuana appears to occupy fourth place in worldwide popularity among the mind-affecting drugs—preceded only by caffeine, nicotine, and alcohol....

The first definite record of the marijuana plant in the New World dates from 1545 A.D., when the Spaniards introduced it into Chile. It has been suggested, however, that African slaves familiar with marijuana as an intoxicant and medicine brought the seeds with them to Brazil even earlier in the sixteenth century.

There is no record that the Pilgrims brought marijuana with them to Plymouth—but the Jamestown settlers did bring the plant to Virginia in 1611, and cultivated it for its fiber. Marijuana was introduced into New England in 1629. From then until after the Civil War, the marijuana plant was a major crop in North America, and played an important role in both colonial and national economic policy. In 1762, "Virginia awarded bounties for hemp culture and manufacture, and imposed penalties upon those who did not produce it."

George Washington was growing hemp at Mount Vernon three years later....

...At various times in the nineteenth century large hemp plantations flourished in Mississippi, Georgia, California, South Carolina, Nebraska, and other states, as well as on Staten Island, New York. The center of nineteenth-century production, however, was in Kentucky, where hemp was introduced in 1775. The invention of the cotton gin and of other cotton and wool machinery, and competition from cheap imported hemp, were major factors in this decline in United States hemp cultivation.

The decline in commercial production did not, however, mean that marijuana became scarce. As late as 1937, the American commercial crop was still estimated at 10,000 acres, much of it in Wisconsin, Illinois, and Kentucky. Four million pounds of marijuana seed a year were being used in bird feed. During World War II commercial cultivation was greatly expanded, at the behest of the United States Department of Agriculture, to meet the shortage of imported hemp for rope....The area of Nebraska land infested with "weed" marijuana was estimated in 1969 at 156,000 acres.

The medicinal use of marijuana in the United States

...Between 1850 and 1937, marijuana was quite widely used in American medical practice for a wide range of conditions. The *United States Pharmacopeia,* which through the generations has maintained a highly selective listing of the country's most widely accepted drugs, admitted marijuana as a recognized medicine in 1850 under the name *Extractum Cannabis* or Extract of Hemp, and listed it until 1942....

To meet the substantial nineteenth- and early twentieth-century medical demand for marijuana, fluid extracts were marketed by

Parke Davis, Squibb, Lilly, Burroughs Wellcome, and other leading firms, and were sold over the counter by drugstores at modest prices....

It was a change in the laws rather than a change in the drug or in human nature that stimulated the large-scale marketing of marijuana for recreational use in the United States. Not until the Eighteenth Amendment and the Volstead Act of 1920 raised the price of alcoholic beverages and made them less convenient to secure and inferior in quality did a substantial commercial trade in marijuana for recreational use spring up.

Evidence for such a trade comes from New York City, where marijuana "tea pads" were established about 1920. They resembled opium dens or speakeasies except that prices were very low; a man could get high for a quarter on marijuana smoked in the pad, or for even less if he bought the marijuana at the door and took it away to smoke. Most of the marijuana, it was said, was harvested from supplies growing wild on Staten Island or in New Jersey and other nearby states; marijuana and hashish imported from North Africa were more potent and cost more. These tea pads were tolerated by the city, much as alcohol speakeasies were tolerated. By the 1930s there were said to be 500 of them in New York City alone.

In 1926 the New Orleans *Item* and *Morning Tribune,* two newspapers under common ownership, published highly sensational exposes of the "menace" of marijuana. They reported that it was coming into New Orleans from Havana, Tampico, and Vera Cruz in large quantities, plus smaller amounts from Texas....

Much of the smuggled marijuana was smoked in New Orleans; but some, it was said, was shipped up the Mississippi and "found its way as far north as Cleveland, Ohio, where a well-known physician said it was smoked in one of the exclusive men's clubs."...

"The first large growing crop in [New Orleans] was found in 1930 and its value estimated at $35,000 to $50,000....In 1936 about 1,200 pounds of bulk weed were seized along with considerable quantities of cigarettes. On one farm, 5½ tons were destroyed and other farms yielded cultivated areas of about 10 acres....One resident of the city was found growing 100 large plants in his backyard." The net effect of eleven years of vigorous law enforcement was summed up by Commissioner Gomila in 1938: "Cigarettes are hard to get and are selling at 30 to 40 cents apiece, which is a relatively high price and a particularly good indication of the effectiveness of the present control." Marijuana smoking, in short, had become endemic in New Orleans—and remains endemic today. What years of law enforcement had accomplished was to raise the price from two for 25 cents to 30 cents or 40 cents apiece—and even this increase might be attributable in part to inflation.

In Colorado, the Denver *News* launched a similar series of sensational marijuana exposes following the pattern set in New Orleans. Mexican laborers imported to till the Colorado beet-sugar fields, it seems, had found Prohibition alcohol very expensive and so had resorted instead to marijuana, bringing their supplies north with them. A Colorado law against marijuana was duly passed in 1929.

These sensational newspaper accounts and early efforts to outlaw marijuana should not, however, be taken as evidence that marijuana smoking was in fact widespread. In 1931 the United States Treasury Department, then responsible for enforcing both the federal antinarcotics and the federal antialcohol laws, indicated that the marijuana exposés in the newspapers were quite possibly exaggerated....

Following the legalization of weak beer in 1933 and the return of hard liquor the following year, the modest, localized popularity of marijuana during the Prohibition years might have declined further. But additional legal developments intervened....

By 1937, forty-six of the forty-eight states as well as the District of Columbia had laws against marijuana. Under most of these state laws, marijuana was subject to the same rigorous penalties applicable to morphine, heroin, and cocaine, and was often erroneously designated a narcotic....

No *medical* testimony in favor of the proposed federal antimarijuana law was presented at the 1937 Congressional hearings. Indeed, the only physician to testify was a representative of the American Medical Association—and he *opposed* the bill. Marijuana, he pointed out, was a recognized medicine in good standing, distributed by leading pharmaceutical firms, and on sale at many pharmacies. At least twenty-eight medicinal products containing marijuana were on the market in 1937.

Although the proposed federal law preserved the right of physicians to prescribe marijuana and of pharmacists to dispense it, an editorial in the *Journal of the American Medical Association* for May 1, 1937, vigorously opposed the legislation.

Who the Death Penalty is For

Number of states that allow capital punishment: 38

Number of times Alabama judges, who are elected, have overridden jury sentences of life without parole and imposed a death penalty: 47

Number of times they have vetoed a jury recommendation of the death penalty in favor of life imprisonment: 5

—American Bar Association Journal, March 1996

❧   ❧   ❧

BEING ON A JURY made me more interested in other trials in general. While I was on the jury for the Aguirre trial, I visited two others. One was the very beginning of a death penalty trial in Santa Fe, where I live. New Mexico is the state where in November of 1986 the outgoing governor, Toney Anaya, had blanket-commuted the sentences of the five men then on the state's Death Row. At the beginning of 1994, there was one man under sentence of death in New Mexico, Terry Clark, convicted of the rape and murder of a nine-year-old girl while out on appeal bond for another conviction involving the molestation of a girl.

The man whose trial I visited, Jerome Martinez, was from a small rural community north of Santa Fe. The newspapers said he had shot and killed a nine-year-old girl with a gun from her house, which he was burglarizing. He was said to be a heroin addict.

The state had offered Martinez a plea bargain: a life sentence, which in New Mexico is 30 years flat with no credit for "good time." He turned it down at the last minute.

His three lawyers from the state Public Defenders' office in Albuquerque presented a great contrast to the nine defense lawyers I had been observing for weeks as a juror. Throughout the proceedings in the Aguirre case, I found the defense lawyers to be serious, hard working, thorough, well-prepared, apparently concerned about their clients and well groomed, day after day.

Of the three defense lawyers in this death penalty case, one had been a prosecutor in Santa Fe for years and one had recently arrived from California. They appeared annoyed at their client for not accepting the plea bargain the state had offered, they were disgruntled at having to try the case, and they were rumpled and informal looking.

Jerome Martinez, their client, was convicted and sentenced to death within two weeks. Santa Fe being a relatively small town, I heard that more was involved in the case than had emerged during the course of the trial. But I did not hear until a year later that the father of the defendant was the grandfather of the victim. In other words, the girl who was killed was the niece of the man who killed her. It was not a stranger who got killed. What were the relationships among the people involved?

Now we have on Death Row in New Mexico someone who the state was willing to offer a plea bargain to—which, in fact, seems to be a common situation for defendants in death penalty cases.

The following readings comment on the death penalty from a variety of perspectives.

Death Row, U.S.A.

NAACP Legal Defense and Educational Fund, Inc., Winter 1998.

Total number of Death Row inmates known to the Legal Defense Fund as of January 1, 1998:

Race of Defendant

White	1,572	(46%)
Black	1,380	(41%)
Latino	263	(8%)

Dispositions since January 1, 1973:

Executions: 432

Race of defendants executed

White	242	(56%)
Black	161	(37%)
Latino	23	(5%)

Race of victims

White	482	(83%)
Black	72	(12%)
Latino	20	(3%)

Convictions or sentences reversed: 1,642

Editor's note: These statistics show clearly that many more Blacks are on Death Rows across the country than their proportion in the population (about 12%).

Subject to Debate

by Katha Pollitt. *The Nation,* September 11, 1995.

FOR THIRTEEN YEARS, Mumia Abu-Jamal sat on death row in Pennsylvania, and not too many people were interested....When people, black and white, argued about whether the justice system targets blacks unfairly, the test cases were Mike Tyson and O.J. Simpson, multimillionaire celebrities defended by flocks of lawyers and accused of crimes against women: not Mumia, whose case actually raises the relevant issues: a police vendetta, a biased judge, a political trial, a ferocious sentence for cop killing, which is a crime against the state....

Still, thirteen years is a long time, and thanks to the tireless efforts of his small band of defenders, little by little Mumia picked up support: the longshoreman's union, locals of transportation workers, service workers, mail handlers, the Association of Black Police Officers, the United Church of Christ, the Quixote Center, Amnesty International. In Europe, where it is not so controversial to hold that racism infects the American judicial system, and where the death penalty has been abolished, there have been big demonstrations, unreported in the mainstream U.S. press. There was a large, spirited one in Philadelphia in August too.

I oppose the death penalty and am disquieted by the questions raised about the original trial.... I would sign a petition opposing the execution of Timothy McVeigh, too—or any of the 3,009 convicted killers on death row, most of whom, guilty or innocent ... have been on the receiving end of a judicial system biased against the black, the poor, the uneducated, and increasingly determined to kill as many of them as quickly as possible. That's not such a radical position.

Reprinted with permission from the September 11, 1995
issue of *The Nation* magazine.

❧ ❧ ❧

The Deadliest D.A.

by Robert M. Morgenthau, District Attorney.
Letter to the Editor, *The New York Times Magazine,* August 13, 1995.

PERHAPS PHILADELPHIANS SHOULD LOOK at the homicide statistics when evaluating their city's aggressive use of the death penalty ("The Deadliest D.A.," by Tina Rosenberg, July 16). I wonder if they know that in Manhattan—a county with a nearly identical population to Philadelphia's and an identical number of homicides (503) in 1990— we reduced the homicide rate without the use of the death penalty.

While Philadelphia's District Attorney has apparently asked for death in virtually every homicide case since her election in 1991, last year Manhattan reported 320 homicides, 21 percent fewer than Philadelphia's 404. Since the death penalty has not deterred homicides, the millions of dollars expended on it would be better spent on solutions—from prisons to drug treatment programs—that *do*. It is fewer homicides and safer streets, not violence in the name of vengeance, that will give citizens the "feeling of control" they deserve.

Reprinted with permission of the author.

❧ ❧ ❧

A Modest Proposal for Executions
by Nat Hentoff, *The Sacramento Bee,* December 18, 1996.

DURING HIS VISIT TO NEW YORK in 1842, Charles Dickens, the journalist, went to the Tombs, the city's aptly named prison. "In the prison yard—this narrow, grave-like place—men are brought out to die," he wrote.

Dickens noted that "the law requires that there be present at this dismal spectacle, the judge, the jury and citizens to the amount of 25. From the community it is hidden."

Executions in New York and all other states with the death penalty are still hidden from the community. In September, the state of New York, for example, re-instituted the death penalty, although its murder rate was less than that of most states that already had executioners on the payroll. The people wanted finality, and the new governor, George Pataki, was elected on a pledge to get the death machinery going again.

The new rules state that the prisoner shall be terminated in a "suitable and efficient facility, enclosed from public view.... That facility shall contain the apparatus and equipment necessary for the carrying out of executions by [lethal] injection."

Before 1835, executions in New York were open to the public, but they were then moved inside prison walls. As time went on, the jury and the judge who presided over the trial were no longer required to attend. And to further make the killings impersonal—under the new procedures in New York—the final disposition of the prisoner is done by what the law describes as "execution technicians whose names ... shall never be disclosed."

Although capital punishment is administered in the name of the public, and much of the public would not feel fulfilled without it, the execution ceremonies in New York and elsewhere are all performed outside the view of the general public.

It is highly unlikely that there will again be public executions. Such spectacles, it is said, coarsen the citizenry. But there is another way in which those people most directly responsible for making the final judgment can see the end of the story.

Jeremy Epstein, a former assistant U.S. attorney, is head of litigation at New York's Shearman & Sterling and has handled death penalty cases.

In a recent issue of the *National Law Journal,* Epstein proposes that "New York should reinstate the practice requiring the presence of the judge and jury at executions—as was the practice when Charles Dickens visited the Tombs in 1842." And, I would add, in every state with capital punishment, the judge and jury at the trial of the condemned should be present to say good-bye to the prisoner.

"Requiring the presence of judge and jury at all executions would have many beneficial consequences," Epstein said. "It would focus the attention of those imposing the punishment on the gravity of their act. Jurors could not simply depart from the courtroom and leave the state with the unpleasant task of disposing of the defendant." Epstein coolly adds that "if the experience of witnessing an execution is traumatic and leaves an impression that lasts a lifetime, so much the better. The impact of the act is at least as traumatic on the defendant and will also last for what remains of his life."

There is further logic in the Epstein proposal: "One of the purposes of any penal system is to teach that acts have consequences: Crime, in short, leads to punishment. It is no less fitting that judge and jury understand that their acts, taken in the isolation of the courtroom, have consequences that reverberate far beyond it."

Epstein, making another point—in the spirit of some of Charles Dickens' novels—says that "a judge and jury's involvement in the actual execution might also remove from public debate some of the detachment with which the death penalty is beginning to be viewed.

"Although executions are not yet a daily occurrence in the United States," he notes, "they are taking place with far greater frequency and are at the point of being considered routine. The taking of a human life by the state should never be considered a routine event, no matter how often it occurs."

Accordingly, I would add, executions should be televised so that not only judges and juries will see the consequences of the death penalty—which would not have been enacted without the cheerleading of much of the citizenry.

No commentary would be necessary for these public service documentaries. And C-SPAN could make a choice of which executions to cover....

I would also hope that the audiences in the death chamber itself would occasionally include some of the legislators who have passed death-penalty bills—and the governors who have signed the death warrants.

Sacrifice of Criminals as a Sacred Rite

by Hans Broeckman, *National Catholic Reporter,* April 12, 1996.

NOTHING IS MORE CHALLENGING than convincing teenage boys of the evil of capital punishment. Generally, I have met with frustration in my attempts to reach my students. I never thought Julius Caesar, a warrior and pagan, could serve us as a guiding star.

Recently, while my freshman class and I read excerpts of Caesar's Gallic Wars, we came across the account of a fascinating custom among ancient Celtic tribes. Whether his account of Celtic religion is accurate has been disputed, but Caesar writes how the tribes were willing to sacrifice human life to save another human life and how they built large altars to immolate their victims. The tribes believed the gods were more pleased with the sacrifice of criminals, but even the innocent were punished if "a supply of a criminal kind is lacking."

We discussed from a historical perspective the need for societies to restore order in their relationship with their gods. I mentioned how for us the sacrifice of the Mass was a participation in the real sacrifice of Jesus, made to restore that relationship permanently. A student quickly pointed out the similarity between the execution of Jesus and the sacrifice of the Celtic tribes. But another saw the great difference: Jesus was both victim and sacrificer, priest and sacrament. He chose to sacrifice himself for us and was not coerced as a substitute.

We wondered what makes us engage in the ritual sacrifice of murderers and criminals. Do we also believe that our God will be pleased with the sacrifice of criminals? Do we hope somehow to establish lasting order through these sacrifices, to win God's grace by offering up our murderers?

Certainly, supporters of the death penalty place hopes in it that are religious. No evidence suggests it deters crime. For the supporter of the death penalty, it is an act of symbolism, a sacrament of death that will restore society and allow us to live righteous lives. The public's right to watch but not have the priest's duty to kill the victim, the "participation" on television, these aspects are typical of sacrifice. Part of us needs these killings, but we do not want the miasma of blood.

The paradox of capital punishment is that our sacrificial killing of the victim is in every case more deliberate, more planned, more public, more steady, more ritualistic than the murder committed by the victim. The gas chamber and electric chair have become our new altars: places where we commit killings ritually to appease our God and restore our world.

The freshmen began to see how our sacrificial killing is not pleasing to our God and is predicated on those dark areas of our souls that haunt us and arose in us out of our fear of an evil god. Even the liberation of a true sacrifice of love, available and eternally repeatable, has not slaked the thirst of our ancestors. The thirst is real, but the sacrament of death we are choosing is as abhorrent now as it was to Caesar.

Reprinted with permission of the author.

PART II

What Juries Do

FIVE

The Value of Juries

*Women were barred from jury duty
in many states until the 1970s.*

—Associated Press, August 20, 1995

🌾　🌾　🌾

DURING THE TRIAL, when people would ask me "What's new?" and I would mention that I was on a jury, a common reaction would be "Oh, poor you—couldn't you get off?" Maybe I could have, but I didn't want to.

Reasonable Doubt

After four months of testimony and days of rebuttal and its response, called surrebuttal, and the judge reading the jury instructions to us as rapidly as possible, we finally got to closing arguments. That was kind of scary, because it meant that the courtroom portion of the proceedings was coming to an end. We jurors would soon no longer be silent and passive observers. In the jury room we would be active, as the main players in evaluating the meaning of what had been going on in the courtroom all this time.

As far as I was concerned, all of the attorneys spoke too long during their final remarks. The prosecution repeated its familiar message: there was a mountain of evidence all clearly indicating that the defendants were guilty as charged. The defense attorneys spoke about their individual clients and also about what "reasonable doubt" is. That was very important since in order to find their clients guilty, the jury had to find the evidence to be "beyond a reasonable doubt." How sure do you have to be to find something true beyond a reasonable doubt?

The defense attorneys must have gone to the same workshop at a lawyers' conference; most of them had little stories to illustrate what reasonable doubt is—like the judgment of a reasonable person at a stop sign, or being careful to test each plank as you walk across a rope-and-board bridge above a chasm. The lawyers also used props, for example the sketch of a house, with more and more red cracks drawn on it and breaking a raw egg into a wastebasket to show that the government's case was like Humpty Dumpty and couldn't be put together.

One of the defense attorneys was eloquent. At the end of his speech, he told us that the jury represented a "buffer zone" between the U.S. government and his client. He asked us to walk with the defendant "down a road less traveled" and not to let "the awesome power of the government divert us from that path." If there was not sufficient evidence to find his client guilty, he urged us "not to surrender our honest convictions." He told us to "stand strong, stand resolute."

That speech helped to sustain me through what turned out to be two long months of jury deliberations.

Juries have a long history, with origins much older than the United States itself. Their utility has been the subject of intense debate, pro and con. These readings mention some common viewpoints.

※ ※ ※

The Guarantees of a Jury

From *Duncan v. Louisiana,* 391 U.S. 145 (1968).

THE GUARANTEES OF A JURY in the Federal and State Constitutions reflect a profound judgment about the way in which law should
be enforced and justice administered. A right to jury trial is granted
to criminal defendants in order to prevent oppression by the government. Providing an accused with the right to be tried by a jury of his
peers gave him an inestimable safeguard against the corrupt or over-
zealous prosecutor and against the compliant, biased or eccentric
judge. If the defendant preferred the commonsense judgment of a
jury to the more tutored but perhaps less sympathetic reaction of the
single judge, he was to have it. Beyond this, the jury trial provisions
in Federal and State Constitutions reflect a fundamental decision
about the exercise of official power—a reluctance to entrust plenary
powers over the life and liberty of the citizen to one judge or to a
group of judges. Fear of unchecked power, so typical of our State
and Federal Governments in other respects, found expression in the
criminal law in this insistence upon community participation in the
determination of guilt or innocence. The deep commitment of the
Nation to the right of jury trial in serious criminal cases as a defense
against arbitrary law enforcement qualifies for protection under the
Due Process Clause of the Fourteenth Amendment, and must therefore be respected by the States.

※ ※ ※

Life and Language in Court

by Robin Tolmach Lakoff. From *Talking Power: The Politics of Language* (BasicBooks, 1990).

...THE REAL POWER in the courtroom belongs to the jury, the
silent party to the courtroom conversation. Not only is the jury silent,
but it is also an outsider uneducated in the law, all of which would nor-

mally ensure powerlessness. It is extraordinary when you think of it that we are willing to entrust such a responsibility—even including life and death—to a group of people who are, after all, only *us*....What a monumental responsibility to place on ordinary people with no special training...The jury is truly closer in spirit to the defendant than a judge would be....When the judge is...on the bench, the jury is brought in, and court is now really in session. The jury must see only order. The jury is the last to enter and the first to leave the courtroom, which the jurors always do *en masse* from or to the jury room. The message conveyed to all present is that the jury creates the trial.

Reprinted with permission of the author.

❦ ❦ ❦

My Men and Women of the Year

by Alexander Cockburn, *Liberal Opinion Week*, January 8, 1996.

I OFFER 12 PEOPLE as Men and Women of the Year. Their names vary. They may be male or female, white or black. Many of them approach their distinction with reluctance. A few in particular have abuse showered upon them. I give you the jury: the last, best bulwark of ordinary folk.

The jury has all the right enemies. One of my neighbors is in the midst of negotiating a contract with big shopping mall operators for a cafe on one of their premises in central California. The mall operators' proposed lease agreement stipulates that in the event of any dispute both parties renounce the right to trial by jury.

The reason is simple. Big money can control any process except the one presided over by a jury. This is why, for over a hundred years, big business has tried to erode the power of juries in civil tort cases, with a particularly intensive push for "reform" in the present Congress, with Speaker Gingrich enthusiastically supporting curtailment of jury powers. Those traditional accomplices of Big Business, the liberal elites, don't like juries either. Juries are unpredictable, fractious and mostly composed of people despised by these elites as—to use the patronizing words of the English Common Law commissioners of 1853—"unaccustomed to severe intellectual exercise of protracted thought."...

Such genuine conservatives as exist in the country tend to support the jury system and call for state constitutions to have judges advise juries as to their inherent powers to decide each case on the basis of the facts laid before them and according to the dictates of their conscience. An explicit judicial advisory on jury powers is now being fought for by the Fully Informed Jury movement.

Most of my fellow leftists, I regret to say, are as frightened of jury powers as are the liberal elites. Remind them that juries acquitted John Peter Zenger, Susan B. Anthony, and those Northerners harboring runaway slaves before the Civil War, and their eyes glaze. They too believe in the wisdom of the elites, even though Harvard professors in the late 19th century were asserting the biological affinity of black people to chimpanzees at exactly the same time as jurors were resisting infamy.

Why is it that when executive power is abused, we end up with an affirmation and often an increase in that executive power? When a U.S. president blunders or commits an illegal act, no one suggests that the presidency be abolished. When a professor is caught in acts of plagiarism, no one calls for repeal of the tenure system. But when democratic power blunders or is abused there are prompt calls for the institution to be abolished.

Protesting the (entirely reasonable) decision of the O.J. Simpson jury, that bastion of liberal elitism, *The New Republic*, called for the abolition of the jury system, with Michael Lind claiming—ignorantly—that it was nothing but a barbaric Viking relic.

Shoulder to shoulder with Lind here is California Gov. Pete Wilson heartily endorsing the proposition, on the ballot next year, ending the unanimity rule for juries in state courts.

But the partial neutering of the jury by the introduction of the

10-2 or the 9-3 verdict leads, down the road, to further attrition and ultimately to the destruction of jury power.

A famous English judge, Lord Devlin, gave some lectures on the jury in the mid 1950s in the course of which he said this:

"The malady that sooner or later affects most men of a profession is that they tend to construct a mystique that cuts them off from the common man. Judges, as much as any other professional, need constantly to remind themselves of that....Trial by jury (has) ensured that Englishmen got the sort of justice they liked and not the sort of justice that the government or the lawyers or any body of experts thought was good for them....Trial by jury...gives protection against laws which the ordinary man may regard as harsh and oppressive." No tyrant, Devlin went on, "could afford to leave a subject's freedom in the hands of 12 of his countrymen. So trial by jury is more than an instrument of justice and more than one wheel of the Constitution. It is the lamp that shows that freedom lives."

Reprinted with permission of Creators Syndicate.

ᴡ ᴡ ᴡ

Jury Competence
by Valerie P. Hans and Neil Vidmar. From *Judging the Jury* (Plenum Publishing Corporation, 1986).

...THE CRITICS WHO ARGUE that juries are incompetent are really making a comparative judgment with a particular alternative in mind. After all, few people, if any, would argue that trials are unnecessary, and few would want to see trial outcomes determined by the ordeal or by a flip of a coin. The alternative to the jury is to have the judge try the case alone and render the verdict. (Another alternative could be a panel of judges or a mixed panel composed of judges and lay persons as is the practice in some of the legal systems of Europe; but this alternative is seldom considered in Anglo-American jurisprudence.) The position of critics opposed to the jury, therefore, is this: A judge, who has formal training and experience in law and in the logic of evidence, is far more likely than twelve men and women taken off the street to be able to decide a case accurately and according to the law....

In the 1950s, the University of Chicago Law School's Jury Project undertook the task of discovering if and how juries differed from judges. The logic of their research strategy was simple. Since judges preside over the trial and hear the same evidence as the jury, one need only to ask the judge how he or she would have decided the case and then compare the judge's hypothetical verdict with the actual decision of the jury. The researchers enlisted over 500 judges across the United States to participate in the study. The judges eventually returned data on 3576 criminal trials. At the end of each trial the judge filled out a detailed questionnaire. The completed questionnaire described the nature of the case, the nature of the evidence, the jury's verdict, the verdict that the judge would have reached, reasons why the judge differed with the jury (if he or she differed), and other relevant information. The results were published by Professors Harry Kalven and Hans Zeisel in a 1966 book entitled *The American Jury*. It is a landmark study that is continuously discussed in the literature of social science and law. It has been frequently cited in Supreme Court and lower court decisions as well.

Professors Kalven and Zeisel compared the differences in the number of convictions and acquittals between judges and jurors. In any criminal trial, the jury is faced with one of two alternative decisions: to acquit or to convict the defendant. The judge has the same two alternatives. Kalven and Zeisel simply compared the number of times the judge and jury agreed or disagreed in a sample of 3576 trials. The results of their study show that the judge and jury agreed on the verdict 78% of the time. In 64% of the cases both judge and jury agreed that the defendant was guilty, and in 14% they agreed that the defendant should be acquitted (64% + 14% = 78%). But these figures mean that the judge and jury disagreed on the remaining 22% of cases. The nature of the disagreement was interesting. Had the judges tried the cases themselves, that is, without a jury, there would have been substantially more convictions. Specifically, in 19% of the trials the jury acquitted when the judge would have said guilty. In only 3% of the cases did the jury convict when the judge would have acquitted (19% + 3% = 22%) . In brief, judge and jury disagreed on the verdict in one trial out of every five; and when they did, in the vast proportion of the times the jury was more lenient than the judge....

What then does account for the judge/jury disagreement? A number of factors were found to explain why jurors were often more lenient than judges. If the defendant had no prior criminal record, the jurors were likely to give him or her the benefit of the doubt. The jury was also more likely to interpret the standard of "beyond a reasonable doubt" in the defendant's favor. Sometimes the disagreement arose because of jury sympathy toward the defendant. Sometimes they apparently disagreed with the law itself....

The American Jury concluded that it was not jury incompetence that caused disagreement between judge and jury....

Reprinted with permission of Plenum Publishing Corporation from *Judging the Jury*, by Hans & Vidmar. Copyright 1986 by Plenum Publishing Corporation.

❦   ❦   ❦

The Strength of the Jury System

From *Huffman & Huffman* v. *U.S.,* 297 F.2d 754, (CA 5th 1962).

THE STRENGTH OF THE JURY system is its absolute, real, actual independence. It must take its instruction on the law from the judge, but the jury alone determines the facts. It is simply not legally correct that some jury must sometime decide that the defendant is "Guilty" or "Not Guilty." The fact is, as history reminds us, a succession of juries may legitimately fail to agree until, at long last, the prosecution gives up. But such juries, perhaps more courageous than any other, have performed their useful, vital function in our system. This is the kind of independence which should be encouraged. It is in this independence that liberty is secured.

Two Major Changes

From the Foreword by Hans Zeisel to *Judging the Jury* (Plenum Publishing Corporation, 1986).

...THE JURY IS UNDERGOING two major changes. One change, the democratic broadening of the reservoir from which jurors are recruited, was highly beneficial. The other change, the manifold reductions of the jury's size has not been helpful.

...Lifting the unanimity requirement has been another form of reducing the jury's size.

The price of these economies is lesser representation of the community, and a greater likelihood of a wrong verdict, because the collective wisdom of the 6 jurors is less than that of 12...

The criminal jury is being diminished by a different threat. Unknown to the general public, some jurisdictions have reduced jury trials to the danger point. In one of our major cities, the share of jury trials of all dispositions after felony arrest has sunk to 2 percent. This is the result of a sentencing policy that discourages jury trial by giving defendants after conviction by a jury on the average more than twice the sentence they had been offered (and refused) for a guilty plea.

Despite the jury's deep roots in the Constitution and in the consciousness of the people, it remains an embattled institution. Any systematic clipping of the jury's wings is dangerous; curtailments that reduce the jury's performance swell the ranks of its critics, and thus start a vicious circle....

SIX

How Juries Make Decisions

A mistrial from a hung jury is a safeguard to liberty;
in many areas it is the sole means by which one or a few
may stand out against an overwhelming contemporary public
sentiment. Nothing should interfere with its exercise.

—*Huffman & Huffman* v. *U.S.*, 297 F.2d 754 (CA 5th 1962)

❧   ❧   ❧

THE CONSPIRACY COUNT of the indictment that the jury in the Aguirre case received was accompanied by a list of 23 "overt acts" headed "In furtherance of the conspiracy and to achieve the objects thereof, the defendants and their co-conspirators, known and unknown to the grand jury, committed and caused to be committed the following overt acts in the District of New Mexico and elsewhere." A number of these overt acts also appeared later as separate counts. The evidence linking the defendants to these acts appeared to many on the jury to be thin, at best. We had been provided with forms to use to communicate—only in writing—with "the court." On Friday, June 10, 1994, we sent a note to the judge that read: "Must the overt act or acts in which a defendant is named be found to be true for the defendant named in that overt act to be found to be a co-conspirator in the Count II conspiracy?"

On Tuesday, June 14, the reply came back: "The answer is no.

Please re-read instructions 8 E to I." We had already read and re-read the instructions repeatedly. The judge's note seemed to mean participation in particular overt acts did not need to be proven. Not having the necessity to prove participation in overt acts made it a lot easier for jurors to vote defendants "guilty" as members of the conspiracy according to their prejudices and opinions, rather than according to the evidence.

That was the second time that we had asked for clarification from the judge. Both times reflected the jury's lack of agreement in interpretation of the instructions; neither question received a helpful answer.

The case went to the jury Thursday, May 5, and the jury returned the verdict Tuesday, July 12. We deliberated from nine in the morning until four in the afternoon, Monday through Thursday and from nine to three on Fridays (during the trial we had not had court on Fridays). During deliberations we all ate lunch together under the watchful eyes of our two deputy marshals. We recessed the week of Memorial Day at the request of several of the younger jurors who had planned family vacations for that time.

We jurors, about half of whom lived from one to four hours' drive away, had our lives completely disrupted by having to stay overnight during the week in Albuquerque. For that we got $94 a night, no receipts required; good money for working people in New Mexico. This was in addition to the $40 (for the first thirty days and then $50 per day) for jury service itself, for those who did not just continue the pay from their jobs, plus mileage.

Weighing the Evidence

We were clearly instructed to "weigh the evidence." How we did that depended on who we were and the background and life experiences we brought to the jury. For example, the defendant who worked as a public elementary school janitor had as character witnesses his school principal, school librarian and school nurse. As a public school teacher, that really made an impression on me. In my experience, public school principals do not take risks with public opinion. Yet here he was, going out of his way to say totally positive things about this defendant. That testimony did not seem to impress the other jurors.

Composition of Our Jury

We were a varied group, reflecting our diverse community. The one person on our jury who I feel most sure might have voted differently than she did was the woman who announced at the beginning that she would not hang the jury. We turned out to be so split, however, that the changing of her vote would not have changed the final verdict on any of the 31 counts.

This same woman was also the only person, among the half dozen or so of us who took extensive notes, whose notes did not track with the others; they seemed incomplete and inaccurate. She was also the one who was adamant about dismantling the prosecution's organization of its many exhibits. Rather than keep them arranged by exhibit numbers, she re-arranged them in separate boxes marked with each defendant's name, even though many of the papers applied to more than one defendant. Several times individual exhibits were extremely hard to find. Almost until the end of deliberations this juror would be sorting through the exhibits and moving them around rather than sitting at the table, examining the exhibits concerning a particular count, and discussing them with the rest of us. Several times she threatened to go to the judge and say this was too much for us, or that she was going to walk out.

Also on the jury was a woman who had said several times during the trial that she thought people ought to be considered guilty until proven innocent. She also thought that perhaps the reason so many of us were suffering various kinds of stress symptoms was *brujeria,* or witchcraft, which might be coming from Mexico. She and one other juror acted frightened by the "reputation" of the defendants. These two jurors appeared concerned that the defendants would hurt them or would come after them in some way.

Another juror seemed influenced during deliberations by memories of an alcoholic mother and a marijuana-smoking niece and by the hardships and troubles both had caused. This was the only juror who had been on a jury before.

There was also a woman who felt that God had been displeased by what the defendants were alleged to have done. She, perhaps even more than the others, took very seriously her responsibilities as a juror, to the point of not asking for a break when her ill father died during the trial. She is the one who saw to it that we started deliberations every morning with a silent prayer, holding hands around the table.

Three jurors voted "not guilty" across the board: One was silent during deliberations, the other two were among the most talkative. One of the talkative ones was particularly charming, repeatedly stating that she would be happy to change her vote if others would just show her the evidence for their position, and that we needed more time to consider our verdicts.

One of the four pro-conviction jurors and one juror most adamant for "not guilty" were, by demographic characteristics, very much the same. Both were Anglo, single and childless, had post-bachelor's college degrees, liked to read, were well-informed, had traveled a good deal and came from relatively "liberal" and "professional" backgrounds. There was about 15 years' difference in their ages. During the trial they enjoyed talking with each other and exchanging the names of favorite authors and restaurants. The younger one also was a Harley-Davidson fan.

During deliberations, there were several running disagreements. Some jurors felt criticized when others disagreed with them. Until near the end, however, when we began to vote on the charges against the alleged ringleader, Gabe, and it became clearer that we were not going to reach agreement, there were many pleasantries, much kidding around, and some socializing outside of the jury room. At least half of the jurors went, sometimes together, to play bingo during off-jury hours and a number also went to Las Vegas when the trial was in recess.

The Length of Jury Deliberations

One of the unusual features of this trial was the length of the jury deliberations—two months. This wasn't because we were explicitly arguing with each other, at least for the first six weeks. The jurors all took their responsibilities extremely seriously. There was agreement that the prosecutors' case, although lengthy and detailed, was not clear and there was great interest in going through our notes and exhibits and attempting to put the prosecution's case together for them. This took three weeks.

That process made it clearer than ever that the testimony of the 25 or so informant witnesses was vague, sometimes inconsistent and sometimes contradictory. We spent an additional two weeks attempting to organize and clarify their testimony—what they had said and not said as it related to the charges we were to vote on.

Throughout deliberations, one of the greatest tensions among the jurors was how long we should take—what the importance of acting promptly was and how many hours we should work each day. The split did not follow our position on the issues. Generally the Albuquerque-area jurors, younger and closer to home, were for working less. The older jurors were more in favor of completing their assignment in a timely manner; furthermore, when finished, they would finally be able to live at home again.

As deliberations began, I found the process more comfortable than that of four months of endless silent listening in the jury box. The courtroom was very formal and rather intimidating. As a long-time workshop presenter, I found being in a meeting of a dozen people trying to share information and opinions to reach a consensus on issues a familiar one. It made me laugh when I realized that, because of the ages and gender of the jurors, there were similarities with the menopause workshops I had been giving for years.

These articles on jury deliberations reflect the variety of those deliberations.

Inside the Jury Room

by Valerie P. Hans and Neil Vidmar. From *Judging the Jury* (Plenum Publishing Corporation, 1986).

...EVEN BEFORE AN ACTUAL JURY retires to the privacy of the jury room, forces unconnected with the evidence presented at the trial are at work that will affect the goings-on of deliberation. Over the course of the trial, the jury undergoes a metamorphosis from a collection of twelve individuals into an enclosed group. Alliances between members develop during recesses, over lunches, while carpooling, and even as a result of the location of the jurors' assigned seats. The social forces that promote this transformation are especially strong during an extended trial.

However, during the presentation of evidence, jurors are forbidden to discuss the one thing that is on everybody's mind: the case itself. So jurors explore similarities and differences among themselves by discussing "safe" topics like food, politics, current events, or sports. Views on these subjects provide clues to the jurors about the perspectives of their fellow jury members on the forbidden topic, the trial....

Once the case is concluded and the jury is sent off to deliberate, the first item of business is selecting a group leader, a foreman or forewoman....Usually only a few minutes is devoted to the process. Often, one juror will ask: "Who wants to be foreman?" A juror may nominate himself or herself or agree to the task when his or her name is suggested, usually by someone he or she has formed an alliance with during the trial. Interestingly, the first person nominated typically becomes foreperson.

Even though selecting a foreperson takes only a few minutes, the process is not as unstructured as it appears. Status in the jury room mirrors status in the outside world. More often than not, the chance of leading the jury is highest for a white male with a college degree or postgraduate work, in a high-status occupation, and with previous jury service. Women are selected as the foreperson much less frequently than one would expect from their numbers on the jury....Studies of selecting the foreperson in mock juries have revealed other interesting patterns. For example, whoever speaks first at the start of the deliberations is likely to be picked to lead the jury. Whoever sits at the head of the table (as opposed to the sides) is likely to be picked....

That isn't to say that only high-status men lead juries. Indeed, a celebrated counterinstance occurred in the trial of black Communist Angela Davis. The jury selected a woman, Mary Timothy.... Even though women are not typically chosen as leaders of juries, the selection of Mary Timothy was probably no accident. Compared to a number of the other jurors, she had high external status. A college graduate, she worked at Stanford University carrying out medical research. Moreover, her husband was a lawyer. In addition, as you will see, she had already formed alliances during the trial with vocal members of the group. Witness, below, the support of Bob, a high-status male, who spoke first in the deliberations to nominate her. On her own, however, she had already shown her inclination for leadership by photocopying a suggested outline for jury deliberations and distributing copies to other jurors at an earlier stage of the trial. In Mary Timothy's account of the jury deliberation, she described how she was picked as foreperson, which gives us an intriguing glimpse into the selection process.

> No one wanted to sit down. No one knew how to get started. With all the others milling around the room, I wondered where I should sit....I went over to get a drink of water and when I straightened up from the fountain, the rest of the group had moved en masse to the table and were pulling out chairs and taking seats. I joined them and found that the only empty chair was at the head of the table. Each of the jurors had instinctively avoided that seat. I hesitated. I didn't want it to appear that I was assuming that I would be selected, or that I wanted the job, or that this was a fixed election.
>
> As I stood looking around the table, trying to avoid sitting in the only empty chair, Bob called out, "Mary, come sit here!" and he stood at the head of the table pulling out that chair for me to use.

I sat down and he remained standing and started to speak, "I would ask the group's indulgence because I am the senior member, and would you allow me the honor of speaking first as we start our deliberations?"

There was no objection—in fact, everyone seemed pleased that he took the initiative and got things moving. He spoke briefly, saying that he knew that we were all aware of the importance of the role that we, as jurors, were playing in this historic trial and that he felt it was time to add another footnote to history and select a woman to be foreman of this jury—and he would suggest that Mary Timothy be the one.

A number of jurors assented immediately. But one juror objected and nominated Jim, an Annapolis graduate and ex-Navy officer who worked as an airport flight controller. A secret ballot produced eight votes for Mary and four for Jim, hence Mary Timothy became the foreperson. Diplomatically, after the vote, Mary leaned over to Jim and asked him to stay beside her and help her with any difficult spots she couldn't handle alone. He agreed.

Occasionally, getting started proves to be a challenge for juries....When finally it comes time to act, judges do not give jurors much guidance on how they are supposed to go about their task....Juries may begin their deliberations in a diverse number of ways. A popular option is to poll the jury. Polling occurs most frequently at the beginning and toward the end of deliberation. It's done in several ways, as a Chicago study of mock juries deciding a civil suit illustrated. In that study, over one-third of the juries used the *go-around,* in which jurors in turn announced their verdict preferences. Another third used *secret ballots.* Two other ways, used less frequently and typically employed later in the deliberations, were a *show of hands* and *verbal dissent,* in which only those jurors who opposed a motion or vote spoke up. When groups were far from being unanimous, the jurors typically used the go-around and secret ballots. But as groups approached unanimity, they employed a show of hands and verbal dissent more frequently.

Whichever polling method is used can affect deliberation and even the verdict itself. In the Chicago study, juries who made more use of the secret ballot were more likely to end up with a hung jury. Furthermore, juries that took polls before beginning to deliberate were the fastest to reach their verdicts. Juries that delayed voting until unanimity was reached were the slowest to reach a verdict.

A detailed study of simulated jury deliberations revealed that the manner of beginning the discussion is associated with different styles of deliberation....In the "verdict-driven" deliberations, juries often began with a public ballot. Jurors aligned themselves with others who held similar positions, and embarked on deliberation by citing evidence in support of their positions. Throughout the verdict-driven deliberation, statements about which verdict jurors preferred and polling were frequent. In contrast, the beginning of the "evidence-driven" deliberation was devoted to a general review of the evidence rather than the identification of verdict preferences. Instead of mentioning only facts supportive of their own positions, jurors engaged in a general assessment of the evidence and tried to develop a joint account of the events related to the crime. Polling the jury occurred much later in the deliberation.

...Juries... are rarely unanimous from the start of the deliberation. To reach unanimity, jurors must weigh the strengths and weaknesses of all their different perspectives concerning the evidence. In the first stages of deliberation, jurors generally focus on the trial testimony. Later, they shift to discussion of the judge's instructions on the law, the different verdicts they might reach, and the task of applying the law to the facts. The period of open discussion and conflict is the heart of deliberation. The substance and pace of such discussions, according to jury researchers, seem erratic and disorganized....

Talk of evidence dominates the deliberations. In one study, for example, over half the comments jurors made were devoted to specific testimony or other facts; another quarter concerned the judge's instructions about the law. Jurors mention evidence they feel is important or confusing, solicit various views of the evidence, and confront the perceptions of others regarding the strength of the evidence....

Jurors frequently bring personal knowledge as well as more direct personal experiences to bear on the case at hand....

Research studies show that the amount of group participation is related to the characteristics of the individuals themselves. Just as external status is reflected in the selection of the foreperson of the jury, it is reflected too in who participates the most during deliberation. On the average, men speak more than women. Those with more education and higher-status occupations also tend to dominate the discussion. Likewise, the foreperson, usually male, is regularly one of the most active participants. Research with simulated juries reveals that most juries include several people who virtually never participate in the deliberation. They have little impact on the group decision-making process; their only contribution may be to take part in the balloting. Typically, these low participators are members of large factions, that is, groups of people who share the same verdict preference. Indeed, one of the most striking patterns of participation is that the larger the faction to which a juror belongs, the less likely that juror is to speak. If only one or two jurors represent a certain position, they tend to be very active in the deliberation; but if a large number of jurors espouse a position, they each tend to speak less.

As differences of opinion about the case are brought out into the open, deliberation increasingly focuses on areas of conflict. During the beginning stage of the deliberation, many comments are directed to the group at large. However, subgroups soon develop, composed of jurors who support the same view of the case. As these factions form, the mode and content of conversation shifts. Now, jurors ask one another about the bases for opposing views, challenge the divergent perceptions of other jurors, and justify their own stands. This kind of conflict can make jurors uncomfortable. Not only are they locked in a room with virtual strangers with whom they disagree, but also they must reach consensus or deadlock the jury before they are released....

Most juries begin with a majority favoring one alternative or another—usually conviction. To reach unanimity, the minority will have to either convince everyone else they're wrong or change their own stances to conform with that of the rest. Many people have seen Henry Fonda's brilliant portrayal of the single juror holding out for acquittal against his eleven convicting colleagues in the film *Twelve Angry Men*....Despite the fact that the jury begins its deliberations with eleven of twelve for conviction, the final verdict is a unanimous "not guilty." It makes for a gripping movie, but outcomes like this one almost never occur in real life. Research studies have shown time and again that the best predictor of a jury's final decision is the distribution of opinion among the jurors at the start of the deliberations....Indeed, jurors are much more likely to defect from a smaller faction than a larger one. It is only when a minority juror has initial support, in the form of other jurors with similar views, that the probability that a juror will sway the majority or hang the jury improves.

While the first ballot vote will often reveal what the final verdict will be, it is not completely predetermined. In one study of Wisconsin jurors, about a third of all the jurors said that they had changed their minds at some point during the deliberation. And minorities *do* sometimes prevail. Furthermore, the criminal trial jury operates with what some have called a "leniency bias": Minority jurors arguing for acquittal are more often successful than minority jurors pressing for conviction. This is no doubt due to the high standard of proof required for conviction "beyond a reasonable doubt." Apparently, it is easier to raise a reasonable doubt than to squelch reasonable doubts. Finally, if there are several charges against a defendant in a criminal trial, or the jury is asked to award damages in a civil trial, minority jurors can sometimes effect a compromise on the verdict or the amount of award.

Despite the fact that oftentimes jurors in the minority will eventually conform, they still retain a considerable amount of power during deliberation. Since the typical rule is that juries must be unanimous, the dissenting or unformed opinions create pressures.

...Occasionally, in about one case in twenty, jurors wade unsuccessfully through the morass of evidence and the maze of differing perspectives. Despite repeated and earnest efforts to resolve conflicts, they find the gulf is too wide: They simply cannot reach unanimity. The result is a deadlocked jury.

There is quite possibly no more demoralizing experience for jurors than the inability to reach a verdict, particularly after a lengthy and tiring trial. Often, anger is expressed at the end of the deliberation at the "holdouts" who are preventing the jury from delivering a unanimous verdict. Minority jurors who insist on voting their consciences may still experience the sting of disapproval. Members of hung juries typically report their feeling that they have let the court down.

But have they? Remember that minority jurors will not hang the jury without some initial support. We can infer that trials resulting in hung juries almost always produce some substantial differences of initial opinion among jurors. Jury researcher Hans Zeisel has called the hung jury a treasured, paradoxical phenomenon.

🌿 🌿 🌿

Y'think the Jury System's Good? Read This
by Mike Royko, *The Chicago Tribune*, March 4, 1995.

...THE MOST EDUCATIONAL insight into how juries operate was provided in Chicago by a juror in the original trial of three men for the rape-murder of...a Chicago-area child.

Two of the men...were convicted and sentenced to die. The jury couldn't decide on the third man, and charges against him were dropped.

After 12 years, the case is still bouncing around the courts. It's a legal mess, and a third round of trials is going to be held.

And after 12 years, this is what the juror had to say about his deliberations in a message he posted on a computer bulletin board where a discussion of the case was being held:

"...I was never totally satisfied (even while we were deliberating) that Cruz and Hernandez were the culprits.

"All I could hope for was that the truth would eventually come out during the appeal process, because even though I voted to convict the two, I was far from convinced that Cruz and Hernandez were really guilty and I knew I would never have voted to give them the death penalty based on the 'evidence' heard at the time.

"Most of the jurors felt that the authorities would not have arrested the three if they did not commit the crime. Most of the jurors were convinced of the guilt before the trial started and the procedure was a mere formality.

"The first day of the trial ... the person who was ultimately selected as jury foreman said, 'Well, these guys are here, so they must be guilty of something.'

" ... If I had had more guts, I would have followed what I really believed, which was that there was not enough quality evidence to send Cruz and Hernandez to the electric chair.

" ... I voted to convict only because I did not want to be the only juror who would hold out. Actually there might have been two or three more jurors ... who were not convinced. However, the pressure of the situation was something that is hard to describe.

"During the course of the trial, I kept thinking that it would end in a 'Perry Mason' type of ending, where the guilty person would just come forward and admit to the crime.

"When this did not happen, I got sick to my stomach.

"Again, I felt I could live with myself knowing that sooner or later the real person or persons would be found, and I rationalized this in my decision-making process."

So here we have a man who flatly admits voting to convict two men he thought had not been proved guilty.

Why?

"I live in DuPage County (Ill.), have a family in the county, and I felt I did not want to be the person who would go down in history as the one who let ... murderers go free. I really felt that the appeal process would ultimately get to the truth."

❧   ❧   ❧

On Jury's Suggestion, School Renamed for Black Official

by Associated Press. *Santa Fe New Mexican*, January 16, 1997.

CRISFIELD, MARYLAND—When H. Wayne Whittington claimed he was fired as school superintendent because he is black, the jury did more than just give him his good name back. It suggested the district put that name on a school.

On Wednesday, the district did just that, renaming Crisfield Primary School the H. DeWayne Whittington Primary School.

"It means more to the black community than anything else," said the 65-year old educator, who also was awarded $920,000 in his race-discrimination lawsuit.

Added his attorney Andrew Freeman: "Justice has been done and righteousness prevailed."

For many of the 350 people who crowded into the school gymnasium, it was a fitting tribute on the 68th birthday of the Rev. Martin Luther King, Jr.

🌿 🌿 🌿

Maria del Refugio ("Cuca") Gonzalez Vasquez

by Debbie Nathan. From *Women and Other Aliens: Essays from the U.S.-Mexico Border* (Cinco Puntos Press, 1991).

AT ABOUT 3 O'CLOCK on a hot Friday afternoon in June, 1985, Diana Duran* received a call informing her that Michelle, her two-month old child, was in a hospital emergency room. The baby had just been brought in by two young girls, the caller said, and she wasn't breathing.

Diana is the wife of El Paso attorney Frank Duran, and when she answered the phone she was working at her husband's law office. She thought the call was a hoax. After all, she had phoned the house just a few minutes before and talked to the maid, who said the kids (there were three others besides Michelle) were all fine and that they were playing. Despite her skepticism, Diana rushed from the office in central El Paso and drove to the family's Lower Valley home. When she got there she found all the doors open, the stove on and the maid gone. The other children—six-year old Cristina, four-year-old Anita and one-year-old Frank, Jr.—were upstairs by themselves. Frank and Anita were in the bathroom, smeared with lipstick, and Cristina was yelling, "The maid took Michelle!" Diana packed them into the car and headed for the hospital.

There, she was led to the emergency room, where 10-week-old Michelle lay pierced with IV lines. A doctor again told Diana the baby wasn't breathing on her own. A few minutes later, she went into the waiting room and saw the maid, who was crying. Herself completely distraught, Diana asked what happened. The maid said she'd gone into the bedroom where Michelle was sleeping and found a small baby pillow over her face. Diana kept asking if the baby had fallen. The maid kept saying no. Why, then, Diana asked, hadn't she

---

* The names of the defense and prosecuting attorneys, police and jurors mentioned in this story are authentic. All others have been changed.

called the law office when she found Michelle not breathing? "I don't know your number or name," the maid answered.

HER IGNORANCE ABOUT THE DETAILS of her employer's life was feigned, but for her part, Diana definitely knew very little about the maid, who'd only been working for the Durans a few days. Her name, for instance, was Maria del Refugio Gonzalez Vasquez; but Diana simply called her Cuca, which in Spanish is short for Refugio. She didn't know Cuca's age, either—she figured her to be somewhere between 18 and 20—nor did she know exactly where she was from. Later, the authorities would ascertain that Cuca's hometown was Zaragoza, a small village in the central Mexican state of Zacatecas. She had come up to the border to Juarez a few months before, following a migratory route well traveled by the men and women of her state. The men usually cross the Rio Grande illegally and press farther to jobs in places like San Antonio and Dallas. Women like Cuca, though, don't travel into the U.S. They stay on the border and work as domestics.

Actually, Diana was wrong about her maid's age—the day that Michelle Duran stopped breathing, Cuca was only 17. When she arrived in Juarez in the spring, 1985, she stayed with her cousins and her Aunt Paulina in a tiny cinder block and stucco house in the Galeana colonia on Calle Huajalpa, a dusty rut of a road without street signs, near the Channel 44 TV station towers on the hills that hem Juarez in on its southwest side. Cardboard shacks, goats and human waste snake up and down the local sierra and form the city boundary here. It's a place El Pasoans seldom venture to unless they are missionaries.

Cuca was the third of seven children. Back in her village, she completed only three years or so of elementary school; then, at age 13, she started caring for the house and the younger four siblings. That made her a good candidate for a maid's job, a mainstay occupation for poor, uneducated Latin American country women who migrate to towns. If Cuca had traveled no farther than the nearest big city, Zacatecas, she would have been hired as a live-in domestic or washer woman at $15 or $20 a week. Up on the border though, by 1985, servants' jobs were much better paid, since most young Juarez women were working in the twin plants for $25 or $30. The competition left uppercrust Mexican matrons no alternative but to offer at least that, or more, if they hoped to get and keep a good servant.

Right after she got to Juarez, Cuca was hired by a local family. She worked for them for two months, during which time her *patrona* never knew her last name either; nevertheless, as she later told a jury, she thought Cuca was a "very good girl." This *patrona* had a job herself, and her boss, when he had business in El Paso needing legal attention, dealt with Frank Duran.

The law offices of Francisco Duran, P.C., are on Montana Avenue, near the city art museum. Here, the beautiful old mansions of El Paso's turn-of-the-century ruling class have long since been converted to office space for attorneys wishing to avoid downtown's high rents, but who still want to stay close to the courthouses. Most of the Montana Avenue lawyers are Hispanics by birth. Frank Duran is more than that. He has, for example, gone to court for Trinity Coalition, a community group that lost its government funding to provide low-cost child care after a controversial Mexican-American nationalist took over the leadership. If not a militant, Frank Duran is at least active in legal issues related to Chicano politics.

While Cuca was working in Juarez, Diana Duran gave birth. She was 31, and this was her fourth child in six years. Now, in addition to the 6-year-old, there were three preschoolers, including two in diapers. The Durans were living in a multi-storied, Santa Fe style house, hand-built years ago by El Paso scion Winchester Cooley. It was a veritable hacienda, graced with a parade of arches on the verandah, a pergola in the backyard, fireplaces inside, and dark *vigas* sticking everywhere out of sparkling white stucco. It was the kind of home that, when new, had probably been kept up by two or three

Mexican servants. But that custom had been dead for a few generations. Now there was a big family in the house, but when they decided to hire help, the Durans wanted only one maid. They asked their Juarez client to recommend someone. He in turn asked Cuca's *patrona,* and the deal was done. Cuca sneaked into El Paso illegally, and on May 28, a Tuesday, she began working at the Duran's.

With the move across the international boundary, her earnings probably approximated the typical El Paso live-in maid's salary: room and board plus $40 to $60 a week. In the U.S. interior this might seem scandalously low. But El Paso is a terribly poor city, where many legally resident women earn minimum wage, and $50 is about all they can afford for child care. For upper-middle-class families, though, the prevailing servants' wage is a fantastic windfall that supports mothers' days out, as well as much community volunteerism. But no matter who they work for in El Paso, Mexican maids seldom complain about their pay. After all, it's double the wage in the twin plants and mansions a few blocks south.

Other than the money though, conditions for maids are pretty similar on both sides of the border. Their workday typically begins at breakfast, and includes cooking, sweeping, mopping, vacuuming, making lunch, washing clothes, washing dishes, changing diapers, giving children baths, breaking up their squabbles, taking phone messages, dusting, sorting the laundry, ironing, breaking up more fights and cooking yet another meal. Work doesn't end until the supper dishes are put away. All this for people who aren't your own family, for children who are somebody else's. It's all the same, whether in El Paso or Juarez.

What makes El Paso different is the constant presence of Border Patrol vans. They trundle around neighborhoods and popular shopping areas, making work a prison for undocumented young women. Maids who venture outside their employers' homes constantly fear being picked up and deported; many therefore seldom venture out. In Cuca's case, even if she'd dared leave the house, the

Durans lived in the Lower Valley, but her girlfriends, who were also maids, lived miles away on the East Side.

During the week there was little for her to do but work, and even as maids' jobs go, there was a lot to do. The house was enormous, and of course there were four children. Cuca found herself taking care of everything at once. Diana would later recall scolding her about how "she would carry around Michelle when she would be doing housework. She would sort of just hold her around the waist with one arm and do work with the other hand." Cuca herself would later tell police that a few days after she started working for the Durans, "I was doing housework in one of the rooms downstairs …I had the baby in my left arm, I turned and the baby's head hit the wall. She cried a little but she later quieted down [and] I didn't think it was of a serious nature."

Cuca managed the household on her own for long stretches of time, particularly while Diana was at the office working as her husband's administrative assistant. But weekends promised relief. On Friday, El Paso maids get their wages and the next two days off. On payday evening, while the middle-aged women return to Juarez to visit husbands and children, young, single girls dress up for a night on the town. Toting weekender bags, they perch in glossy flocks at the bus stops, or they board their *patronas'* cars and are chauffeured to friends' houses or to the international bridge. Friday night means dancing, maybe at the clubs on Alameda Avenue. Saturday night there's more partying, and with it a chance to meet a U.S. citizen man, maybe become his *novia,* maybe get married, maybe get legalized. Or if none of that happens, it's a time to meet young Mexican guys, meet friends and just have some fun. Sunday evenings, the migration reverses, and Monday a new week's drudgery begins.

Friday morning, June 7, was the end of Cuca's first full week on the job at the Durans', and she was looking forward to getting off work that Friday evening for the weekend. As usual, it was turning into a hot day. After breakfast, Diana took the older girls to the mall and dropped Frank Jr. off at her father's, leaving Cuca with baby Michelle. After lunch everyone returned home, but Diana almost immediately left for the office. An hour later, Cuca called her new *patrona*. One of her girlfriends was going to be spending that night alone in her employers' home. Cuca wanted to know if she could get off a little early to keep her company.

Diana said no. In fact, she told Cuca, she and Frank had a dinner engagement which preempted the maid's night off. Diana hung up. An hour later, Cuca called again. She wanted to make enchiladas for dinner but there were no corn tortillas in the house. Could the Señora bring some home?

Diana was irritated. She told Cuca to prepare a different meal using the meat and potatoes in the fridge. Then she repeated that Cuca was not allowed time off that evening. And by the way, she asked, how were the children? Fine, Cuca said. Diana hung up again.

Fifteen minutes later, Michelle was unconscious.

AT THE HOSPITAL CUCA kept telling the story about the baby pillow. Diana didn't buy it, especially after another doctor told her Michelle had suffered a blow to the head. Cuca, meanwhile, had left the hospital, apparently after Diana fired her, and had returned sobbing to the Duran house, packed her things and disappeared. Diana spent all night at Michelle's side. On Saturday afternoon the infant was still not breathing on her own, and Diana went to her sister's home, where the other children were staying. While she was there, she later told authorities, the phone rang. It was Cuca's girlfriend, Alicia, demanding that Cuca be given her week's wages. A few minutes later, a man called and said that if Cuca wasn't paid, the Duran house would burn down. Cuca herself then called and began arguing with Diana about the money. "My child is dying!" Diana said, and hung up on Cuca. Shortly afterwards she returned to the hospital. Two hours later, doctors told her Michelle was in a coma.

In the predawn hours of Sunday morning, Diana dictated a

lengthy statement to the police accusing Cuca of injuring Michelle and then trying to hide the truth about what happened. She also recalled heretofore forgotten details, such as that there were two empty Budweisers lying around on Thursday, and it wasn't Frank Duran who drank them. Cuca, meanwhile, left her girlfriend's house and returned to Aunt Paulina's in Juarez.

By Wednesday Michelle was still comatose, and the police wanted Cuca back in El Paso. They contacted her friend Cecilia and asked her to convince Cuca to return for a friendly chat. Cecilia went to Aunt Paulina's and brought Cuca back over the international bridge. It was the first time she'd crossed into the United States legally. Detective Alfonso Medrano was at the immigration office, waiting for her.

Back at the Crimes Against Persons office, Cuca told Medrano the story about the baby pillow and added that she had run with Michelle downstairs, put tap water on her chest and tried mouth-to-mouth resuscitation in a desperate attempt to revive her. She gave a two-page statement, which was typed out in English and translated orally by another Hispanic police officer. She signed her name, with the half-printed, muddy penmanship of the semi-literate. Medrano then arrested her and booked her into the county jail.

According to the young woman who shared her cell, Cuca spent the first days after her arrest poring over religious tracts. Then, on Saturday, she began weeping inconsolably. She asked for a detective, and late that night, she dictated a new statement. In it, she recounted the Friday afternoon call she made to Diana asking to be let off work early, and the frustration she felt when Diana refused to give her the night off. She remembered the second call, the one about the tortillas. She remembered feeling terribly angry, and in the midst of it all, the baby was lying in her bassinet on the kitchen table, crying and crying. Cuca remembered slapping Michelle and throwing her into the bassinet. But the infant still wouldn't stop crying. Cuca remembered putting her hand over the baby's mouth and nose then, and keeping it there. Finally everything was quiet. She remembered turning back to the stove, then hearing a gurgling in the bassinet. She remembered picking up Michelle. She was limp. Cuca tried to revive her, by shaking and shaking her.

Three days after the date of this second statement, Michelle died. Cuca was charged with reckless endangerment as well as with injury to a child—a first degree felony with a maximum sentence of life.

SHE WAS INDIGENT and couldn't afford a lawyer. So as she sat in jail awaiting trial, the state assigned Cuca two young attorneys drawn at random from the public defender pool—Pablo Alvarado and Robert Anchondo. Anchondo remembers the case as one of the hardest he's ever taken. After all, not only was a child dead, but the father was a fellow attorney. "We felt for the Durans," Anchondo says. Nevertheless, his sympathy for Cuca went beyond professional obligation. "She seemed like a very sentimental, innocent girl," he recalls.

He and Alvarado decided that their best defense was two-pronged. First, they would argue that the two policemen's statements were meaningless because Cuca had no comprehension of her right to remain silent, and because she couldn't understand the English text of what she had signed. Second, Michelle's autopsy reports indicated that, whatever else happened to her, the only thing that made her die was the brain trauma caused by being severely shaken.

And now, Cuca had a new story: that while in the bassinet, Michelle had gagged on a piece of food. Alvarado and Anchondo thus planned to argue that, while Cuca admitted shaking the baby, she'd done it not to hurt her, but in a panicked effort to save Michelle from choking.

During the weeks before the trial, the attorneys tried to make things as favorable as possible for their client. They moved to have her confessions quashed. They also requested that when the assistant

D.A.'s referred to Cuca in front of the jury they "refrain from using such language as 'wetback' and 'illegal alien.'" The court denied the first motion and granted the second.

The state, meanwhile, planned to claim that Cuca deliberately hurt Michelle, and that, after putting the infant on her deathbed, she even demanded wages. But whatever the maid's motives had been, at the crux of the case there was inarguably a helpless baby—a dead one. The trial promised to be dramatic.

When it began, though, four months after Michelle Duran died, hardly anybody showed up. Cuca had no family in El Paso and the Durans deliberately stayed away. Even the pensioners who attend trials instead of dollar movies had chosen other entertainment—the divorce proceedings of State District Court Judge and Mrs. John McKellips. In the courtroom where Cuca was to be tried, attorneys went about the humdrum task of picking a jury (the defense was looking for people who themselves had children and maids). Meanwhile, over at the divorce trial, the parties were wrangling over $500,000 worth of community property and a two-story Spanish-style home; Judge McKellips was passing around photos of unkempt bathrooms to prove that his wife was a poor housekeeper, and Mrs. McKellips was accusing the judge of having sex with his campaign chairwoman and contracting genital herpes. For the media and the community, the peccadilloes of the rich were much more glamorous—and, given local conditions, infinitely more escapist—than the common passions of a housemaid and her *patrona* on a hot Friday afternoon.

ULTIMATELY, ANY DRAMA in Cuca's four-day trial was of the abject kind. A jury of mostly Hispanic men and women, mostly blue collar and middle-income people, listened as Assistant D.A. Carole Pennock—petite and impeccably tailored—opened by reciting the details of Cuca's alleged wickedness: her calls to Diana Duran demanding money, the second confession and its talk of slapping, throwing, suffocating and shaking.

Amid all this sat the maid, now known officially as Maria del Refugio Gonzalez Vasquez, and never referred to as "wet" or "illegal." She was barely 18 now and, in her dark-colored, severely cut dress, she could have been a Red Cross girl out to collect donations for a Mexican charity hospital. But she was in court, in the United States, where she understood barely a word of English. A motherly looking woman, the court translator, sat nearby and buffered the States's accusations by converting them to Spanish.

Detective Medrano took the stand. He testified about the jailhouse confession, and Cuca's attorney cross-examined him in a lackluster attempt to show that his client had had no idea what she was signing (even though another officer had translated for her). Then, to explain why Cuca would deliberately have done the things she described in the confession, Diana Duran was sworn in. Stylish, agitated and weeping, she described what happened that afternoon in June, including the conflict between her and Cuca about the maid's night off. Cuca's friend Ceci also testified about the Friday night plans the two girls had made.

A doctor came on to tell the jury how dangerous it is to shake an infant, about how the resulting whiplash causes fatal destruction of the baby's brain and spinal cord. He also showed that, in order to cause such an injury, an adult would have to shake a baby very hard. In his expert opinion, the physician said, such force usually comes from a person who is extremely angry.

By the third day of the trial, the courtroom seemed cavernously empty. There were only two spectators besides myself. One was an elderly black man—apparently he'd tired of the McKellips divorce. The other was a dapper, Clark Gable-esque man who identified himself as an FBI agent and as Michelle Duran's uncle.

"I hate maids," he kept saying during a court recess. "They're ignorant and stupid!" He shook his head, partly in disgust, partly to dislodge a memory that would not go away. "You should have seen her," he said. He spread his hands at waist level. "She was about this big. Plump. And green eyes. Green eyes!" He turned then, and headed into the judge's office, as casually as if it were a public men's room. He didn't come back.

The jury, though, had to stick it out to the end—and it found itself in a quandary. On the one hand, according to panel foreman, Kenneth Jones, no one ever doubted Cuca had done something wrong. When she finally testified that Michelle gagged on a tortilla and that she shook her only to save the baby, the jury thought she was lying and believed that the confession was the more accurate version of what had happened.

The problem was, nobody wanted to punish Cuca. The jurors harbored more animosity towards the cops and the Durans than they did the maid.

"All of them were very hostile to the police testimony," Jones said recently. "It's not that they even cared whether or not [Cuca] was given her rights, or whether what she told them was the truth or not. They just thought the police coerced her into making the confession. For some reason, the Hispanic men and women on the jury were skeptical of police. I guess they've had bad experiences with them in the past."

Jones also noticed that "the Durans are upper-class Hispanics. Most of the jury weren't in their social circles. They couldn't relate to a lady with that kind of money and free time leaving her infant so long in a maid's care and then going off to a social function."

It seemed the jurors were also thinking about their households—Jones said about half of them had their own maids. Still others were remorsefully recalling their own pasts. "What [Cuca] did was intentional," Jones said. "But it was from frustration and could have happened to anyone. How many people are aware of how dangerous shaking a child can be? Most of us on the jury learned this for the first time at the trial. Think of those times you were young, you were babysitting, you got angry...some of us jurors were thinking.

'There but for the grace of God go I.'"

"It was very difficult," Jones remembered. "After we agreed she was guilty, some jurors actually wanted to go back on their decision, simply because she could get a lot of years in the state penitentiary. We finally agreed to the lesser charge of reckless endangerment. Because this being El Paso and most of the jurors being Hispanic, we already knew that, since she was from Mexico, if she got probation she could serve it in Juarez. Which basically means she'd get no punishment at all."

So the jury finally decided to give Cuca a suspended sentence with ten years probation administered by the Mexican authorities. She returned to Aunt Paulina's house in the slum near the mountains. For a time she worked near downtown Juarez, at an outdoor popsicle stand. Later she returned to her village in Zacatecas. Now, every few months, she travels to Juarez with her mother, to buy second-hand clothes to take back and sell to her townspeople.

As for the Durans, they have since left the home where Michelle died—friends say Diana couldn't bear living among the memories of that hot Friday afternoon in June.

Since then, it has become a violation of federal law to hire an undocumented maid. The new policy hasn't changed El Paso much, though. Young women from the interior still cross the river without papers; they still get jobs cleaning houses and minding kids. They still make the same money for the same hard work, still cloister themselves from the Border Patrol, still yearn for their weekends off. And still, undoubtedly, get frustrated with the endless squalling of kids who aren't theirs.

As for Cuca, attorney Anchondo got a call from her a couple of years ago. She was in Juarez and wanted to know if there was any way she could return to El Paso legally. He couldn't help her—she has a criminal record, and to get caught now by Immigration would almost surely land her in federal prison.

But no matter. There'll be others to take her place. "People on the border have always had maids and always will," says jury fore-man Jones. "It's just something that goes with the territory." He remembers the final minutes of Cuca's trial and sentencing. As she rose to leave the court, several jurors surrounded her and shook her hand. They wished her luck and entreated her to use her head, be careful in the future.

Then one Hispanic woman came up. It seems this juror had three or four children herself, and she needed a maid to live in her home, do housework, care for the kids.

She offered Cuca the job.

❧ ❧ ❧

Do You Swear That You Will Well and Truly Try…?
by Barbara Holland, *Smithsonian Magazine,* March 1995.

BRITISH LAWYERS TELL THE STORY of a jury in New South Wales that was considering the matter of some stolen cows, about which the jurors certainly knew more than the court would ever learn. After deliberating, they returned a verdict of "Not guilty, if he returns the cows." The judge was outraged at this insult to the law and threw them back out to think again. Pigheaded and mutinous, they returned with a new verdict, "Not guilty—and he doesn't have to return the cows."

Perhaps justice, if not law, was served.

✌ ✌ ✌

Jurors Go Against 3 Strikes

by Edward J. Boyer, *Los Angeles Times,* June 5, 1996.

THE DEFENDANT'S GUILT was never a serious question. He had been caught red-handed trying to steal three guitars from a Koreatown church sanctuary.

But several jurors who convicted Keith T. Adams were troubled that the church would even press charges. After rendering their verdict, they asked to meet with the judge.

Only then did they learn that the three guitars could send Adams to prison for 25 years to life—his third strike under California's "three strikes" law.

The six jurors in the judge's chambers were stunned. "I mean we were reeling," said one, a woman in her 40s [named Ruth] who lives in Santa Monica. "Twenty-five years for attempting to steal three guitars?" What followed between Adams' conviction and his sentencing is the story of how this juror—herself the victim of armed robbery two months before the trial—set out to temper justice with mercy.

It is the story of how she was haunted, as some California jurors increasingly are, by cases involving relatively minor criminal offenses, wondering but never knowing whether a suspect is on his third "strike."...

The tension underlying the case grew out of the 2-year-old "three strikes" law and the fact that jurors do not know when they deliberate whether a conviction will lead to a sentence far harsher than they had anticipated....

"A lot of us were upset that we were finding a man guilty for what we thought was not a very significant crime," she said. She offered a metaphor: "I thought I was turning on a light bulb, and I was pulling the execution lever."

She was one of three whites on the panel, along with seven

African Americans and two Asian Americans.

Adams...was charged with breaking into the Los Angeles Don Sang Church on West 9th Street in October and trying to steal the guitars—two electric and one acoustic.

Church volunteers and staff members trapped Adams in a corridor between the sanctuary and the church parking lot and held him for police....

A 1988 conviction for an armed home invasion robbery—a strike for each victim—qualified him for "three strikes" prosecution at this trial. After the jurors met with the judge to express their misgivings, with the prosecution and defense attorneys also present, Ruth started making phone calls. She was "trying to find out more about the defendant, more about his history—something to make me feel better about his 25 years in jail."

She talked to Deputy Dist. Atty. Laurie Helfing, who prosecuted the case....She spoke to Earl C. Broady, Jr., Adams' defense attorney. Broady told her that she could write to the trial judge, who still had the option of sentencing the case as a misdemeanor rather than as a felony.

She faxed her letter to Los Angeles Superior Court Judge George Wu on May 20—three days before he was scheduled to sentence Adams....The next day, she called the church's senior pastor, the Rev. Ki Hyung Han....

"I know what [Adams] did is a bad thing," said Kim. "But 25 years? That is too much....In America they give a lot of second chances," Kim said, "We have to give a second chance too."

The case against Adams is what lawyers call a "wobbler," meaning prosecutors could have filed it as a misdemeanor or a felony....

"I've never had a jury express itself as adamantly as in this particular situation," the judge said in an interview. "Frankly, that was a factor I considered. The reverend from the church was also a very strong factor in my mind."

The court can consider jurors' views where punishment is concerned, Wu said. "Their view, while not controlling, is a factor I think I can consider," he said. "I don't mind the jurors commenting. I view jurors as part of the community at large."

Loyola Law School professor Laurie L. Levenson, a former federal prosecutor, said the "three strikes" law has made jurors "more curious now and more concerned" about the consequences of their verdicts. "Therefore, jurors are more uncomfortable if they think they are being used to impose penalties more severe than they think are warranted." On the day of sentencing, Wu spoke from the bench about the letters from Ruth and the Rev. Han. Then, choosing to treat the case as a misdemeanor, he pronounced sentence on Adams: one year in County Jail and three years probation. Adams also has to serve one year for violating parole....

Days later, the Rev. Kim reflected on the case:

"We did a small thing. But that is what a Christian is supposed to do. Dong San means 'hill' in Korean. We want our church to be a hill of healing, a hill of holiness."

SEVEN

Jury Nullification

This disobedience to the fugitive slave law is one of the strongest guarantees for the observance of any just law. You can not trust a people who will keep a law because it is a law, nor dare we distrust a people who will keep a law when it is just.

—Theodore Parker, 1810–1860, Unitarian minister

🌿   🌿   🌿

BEFORE BEING ON THE JURY I was aware that jurors can vote whatever way they want to and do not have to give a reason to anybody why they voted that way.

In the jury room one morning about a month into the trial, one of the jurors brought in a one-page magazine article about "jury nullification" that a friend of hers had sent her. She showed it to another juror and I asked if I could read it too.

Then I said that I thought everyone on the jury should have a copy and that I would be happy to make copies, as I had easy access to a photocopier. The other woman suggested that we just ask the judge's staff to copy it for us. That led to a fuss, as the judge didn't feel it was appropriate for us to see it.

The trial transcript for that day quotes the judge as saying: "I don't want you to change your views on the jury system or judiciary or criminal courts or anything at all during the trial.…Your oath is that you'll make your decision based solely on what you hear in the courtroom.… What I want you to do is keep anything from the outside from coming in during the trial. I want you to come into the courtroom with X amount of knowledge on the judicial system…but I want you to listen to the testimony, listen to my instructions on the law, and then make your decision based on that, not anything you gained from the outside during the trial.…I want you to be…a judicial vacuum during the trial.…"

Needless to say, that made me really curious. Why was the judge so upset? What didn't he want us to know? The woman who brought in the article wrote a note apologizing to the judge. The juror who requested they make copies of it at court said she was afraid they might call a mistrial as a result of her request.

Another incident occurred during jury deliberations in June. As I entered the courthouse in the morning, someone handed me a yellow card from something called the Fully Informed Jury Association (FIJA). I was interested to see it and even more interested when the deputy marshal stopped me as I was entering the jury room to ask me if I'd received one. Apparently, at least some other jurors had and had informed the judge, who confiscated them.

Among the most interesting information about jury nullification to me is its history. It is a very old feature of our judicial system and was an important factor in the trial of William Penn in 1670; today it is part of the constitutions of both Indiana and Maryland. The existence of the power of juries to "nullify" law in any jurisdiction is undisputed. What there appears to be argument about is the right of jurors to be informed of their power to vote their consciences.

The standard judge's instruction to the jury in the Maryland Rules of Procedure (found in *Judging the Jury*) is: "Anything which I say about the law, including any instructions which I may give you, is merely advisory and you are not in any way bound by it. You may feel free to reject my advice on the law and to arrive at your own independent conclusion."

Judging the Jury also points out that a Canadian survey found that 93% of previous jurors are in favor of a "nullification instruction" from the judge.

The four readings included here deal with a topic and a term relatively new to most of us. It is: What should juries do when asked to enforce bad laws?

❧ ❧ ❧

Yellow Card

Fully Informed Jury Association

Trial Jurors: True or False?

1) You can vote to acquit, even if the evidence proves the defendant has broken the law.

   TRUE—your conscience and common sense are even more important than the evidence.

2 You must apply the law as the judge gives it to you, even if you disagree with it.

   FALSE—your job is justice, not obedience, even if you've taken an oath to "follow the law."

3) You can't be punished for your verdict, or made to explain why you voted as you did.

   TRUE—otherwise, instead of having trial by jury, we'd have trial by government.

4) Your only choice as a juror is to find the accused guilty or not guilty as charged.

   FALSE—jurors can find a person guilty of lesser charges, if "contained" in the original.

5) You are not to stop deliberating on a case until you reach a unanimous agreement.

   FALSE—when there is unresolvable disagreement, a hung jury is the appropriate result.

6) You will learn all you need to know about jurors' rights and powers from the judge.

   FALSE—rarely will judges even give you the true information found in this little quiz.

7) You can get better information about your rights and powers as a juror elsewhere.

   TRUE—just telephone "FIJA," the Fully Informed Jury Association, at 1-800-TEL-JURY.

   —Reprinted with permission of FIJA, Helmville, MT.

❦ ❦ ❦

Jury Nullification:
The Top Secret Constitutional Right

by James Joseph Duane, *Litigation,* Summer 1996.

...THE EXISTENCE OF a criminal jury's power to nullify is currently as well settled as any other rule of constitutional law. It is a cornerstone of American criminal procedure. The far more controversial issue—and much more frequently litigated—is that perennial dilemma: What should we tell the kids? Should (or must) the judge tell the jurors anything about their power (or right) to nullify? Should the judge at least allow the defense to tell them? If so, how much should we tell them, and how should we do it? These issues lie at the very core of our criminal justice system, and have been debated by lawyers, journalists, philosophers, and patriots for two centuries. It is therefore ironic that these questions have, at least in recent decades, generated one of the most remarkable displays of unanimity ever orchestrated by state and federal courts on any issue of law in American history.

It would take at most four words to fairly summarize the unanimous consensus of state and federal judges on the idea of telling jurors about their power to nullify: "Forget it. No way." Even while extolling the beauty and majesty of our commitment to the jury's constitutional role as a guardian against tyranny, no state or federal appellate court in decades has held that a trial judge is ever permitted—much less required—to explicitly instruct the jurors on their undisputed power to return a verdict of not guilty in the interests of justice. The federal courts are unanimous and have been for years, e.g., *United States* v. *Manning,* 79 F.3d 212, 219 (1st Cir. 1996) ("a district judge may not instruct the jury as to its power to nullify"). So are the state appellate courts, e.g. *Mouton* v. *Texas,* 923, S.W.2d 219 (Tex. Ct. App. 1996); *Michigan* v. *Demers,* 195 Mich. App. 205, 489 N.W. 2d 173 (Mich. Ct. App. 1992)....

There is a pervasive myth that three states supposedly allow jury nullification instructions: Georgia, Maryland, and Indiana. *See State* v. *Morgan Stanley & Co.*, 194 W.V. 163, 175, 459 S.E.2d 906, 918 n..27 (W.V. 1995); Paul Butler, *Racially Based Jury Nullification: Black Power in the Criminal Justice System*, 105 Yale L.J. 677, 704 n.147 (1995). Some lists also include Oregon. This is presumably because those states have laws or constitutional provisions suggesting that criminal jurors are judges of the law and the facts. But the myth is false. Despite their differing constitutions, all four states have held that a jury has, at most, the power to acquit a guilty man, not the right, and should not be told that it may ignore or nullify the law. *See, e.g., Miller* v. *Georgia*, 260 Ga. 191, 196, 391 S.E.2d 642, 647 (Ga. 1990).

...Case after case has approved jury instructions actually designed to imply that jurors do not have such power at all, or to "instruct the jury on the dimensions of their duty to the exclusion of jury nullification." *United States* v. *Sepulveda*, 15 F.3d 1161, 1190 (1st Cir. 1993). For example, criminal jurors are routinely ordered: "You must follow my instructions on the law, even if you thought the law was different or should be different." Eighth Circuit Pattern Criminal Jury Instruction 3.02 (1991), and "even if you disagree or don't understand the reasons for some of the rules." Federal Judicial Center, Pattern Criminal Jury Instruction 9 (1987).

In extreme cases, this judicial hostility even extends to dishonesty. As Chief Judge Bazelon correctly observed, current law on this topic is tantamount to a "deliberate lack of candor." *United States* v. *Dougherty*, 473 F.2d 1113, 1139 (D.C. Cir. 1972) (dissenting opinion)....

This widespread judicial pattern is highly ironic. The courts have unanimously (and erroneously) refused to let defense attorneys argue for nullification, typically by insisting that the jury has no power to consider what the law should be, and that juries have no lawful task but to decide whether the defendant broke the law. Yet, in a fit of sheer inconsistency, the same federal courts of appeals are also unanimous that it is permissible for prosecutors to urge juries to act as the "conscience of the community" and use their verdict to "send a message" about whether society should be willing to tolerate the defendant's alleged conduct...

In the real world...defendants...make the...request that the jury be told merely of its authority to acquit an accused if a conviction would conflict with their deeply seated sense of morality and justice....

...The jury's power to acquit out of justice or mercy is a constitutionally protected right. If not their right, it is at least the defendant's firmly settled right that he insist on a jury with such power, regardless of whether the proof of his technical legal guilt is literally overwhelming and uncontradicted. *Sullivan* v. *Louisiana,* 508 U.S. 275, 277-82 (1993). Any judicial instructions that would prevent the exercise of this right are unconstitutional....

Contrary to the widespread myth popular among judges, there is no "law" that requires juries to convict every man shown to be technically guilty beyond a reasonable doubt....

Nor does any "law" forbid a jury from pardoning a man who violated an unjust statue, even if an acquittal requires them to ignore the court's instructions on the law. The Constitution does no such thing; it actually protects the jury's right to acquit based on their sense of justice. The penal code does not criminalize such conduct, and would be clearly unconstitutional if it did. Not even the Bible imposes any such rule. *See Deuteronomy* 16:20 ("Follow justice and justice alone")....

Our entire system of justice would be undermined if jurors had the liberty to return a false verdict—even for benign motives of mercy—convicting a defendant of a lesser offense she simply could not have committed, or acquitting her because of some legal defense with absolutely no basis in the evidence.

But that straw man has nothing to do with the typical case of a defendant seeking an instruction on nullification. Such instructions need not suggest that jurors be told they can decide for themselves what the law is or should be, or that they can convict the defendant of some lesser offense (or acquit on the basis of some affirmative defense) with no basis in the facts. Our law does not countenance such contrivances and should not encourage them. But a proper nullification instruction or argument would merely tell the jury the fact—or at least confirm their intuitive suspicion—that our law intentionally allows them the latitude to "refuse to enforce the law's harshness when justice so requires." LaFave and Israel, *Criminal Procedure* Sec. 22.1, at 960....

If a jury refuses to convict a man because of overwhelming feelings of mercy or justice, they are not returning a "false" verdict. A verdict of "not guilty" based on a jury's notions of justice is not affirmatively declaring that he is innocent. (The same is true of an acquittal based on their conclusion that he has only been shown to be probably guilty, but not beyond a reasonable doubt.) The general "not guilty" verdict is merely a shorthand way of allowing the jury to express, for reasons they need not explain, "we do not choose to condemn the accused by pronouncing him guilty."...

If the wording of the (jurors') oath poses some conflict with the jury's constitutional prerogative to nullify, it is clear which one must yield the right of way. Courts simply have no business (much less lawful authority) asking jurors to swear to anything that would violate the Constitution or the jury's deeply held convictions about justice....

...Telling a jury they "must" convict where guilt has been proven beyond a reasonable doubt is a serious misstatement of the law and "an error of the most egregious nature." *Proceedings of the 53rd Jud. Conf. of the D.C. Circuit,* 145 F.R.D. 149, 175 (1992) (Remarks of R. Kenneth Mundy, Esq.). Under our Constitution, by design, a defendant is entitled to have his fate decided by a jury even if the evidence of his guilt is undisputed and decisive. *Sullivan,* 508 U.S. at 277. This is because criminal jurors are entitled to "refuse to convict even though the evidence supported the charge," and any legal system which would strip jurors of that discretion would be "totally alien to our notions of criminal justice." *Gregg* v. *Georgia,* 428 U.S. 153, 199 n.50 (1976)....

If our criminal justice system is to retain some semblance of integrity in the long run, it is vital that we treat jurors with greater candor about the moral and legal contours of their power to nullify. Fortunately, it wouldn't take long. A clear and adequate instruction could be conveyed in a single sentence, explaining that the jury should (not "must") convict anyone proven guilty beyond a reasonable doubt, unless the jurors have a firm belief that a conviction would be fundamentally unjust. Such an instruction would give defendants all the protection they deserve against wrongful prosecution. It would preserve the jury's constitutionally protected veto power over unjust prosecutions. It would minimize the terrible danger of jurors persuading each other that the judge is withholding (or concealing) crucial facts about the way the system is designed to work. And it would, at long last, permit us in good conscience and good faith to ask jurors to take a solemn oath to abide by the court's charge.

Proper instructions on nullification are now quite like sex education to youth in many different ways. There may well have been a time, several decades ago, when it was feasible to avoid both subjects altogether, hoping that our young wards would never even hear much about them until a truly pressing need might arise for them to divine a few things on their own initiative. But now there are precious few secrets about either subject that cannot be found on the Internet and in every major magazine—along with many dangerous falsehoods and half-truths. If we persist in our refusal to confront these delicate topics head on, jurors and children will continue making terrible choices as they learn for themselves what a dangerous thing a little knowledge can be. And in the process, judges and parents alike will continue to lose much of their credibility in the eyes of those who correctly perceive their right to honest guidance from us.

Reprinted by permission of *Litigation*, Summer 1996, Volume 22, Number 4.

🔥 🔥 🔥

Juries and Higher Justice

by Jeffrey Abramson. From *We, The Jury* (BasicBooks, 1994).

The Fact/Law Distinction and the Decline of Jury Nullification

In place of the expansive, inspiring deliberations about law and its relation to justice that characterized the work of the Penn and Zenger juries, modern law invokes the distinction between facts and law to provide jurors with a frequently deadening description of their mission. In virtually every jurisdiction's handbook for jurors, the same mechanical description appears: find the facts, and reach a verdict by applying whatever the judge says about the law to those facts.

But the search for a strict division of labor between jury and judge creates a number of practical problems for trials today....The more we emphasize the remoteness of law from the experience of the average juror, the less credible it is that jurors receive sudden enlightenment on legal matters simply by listening to the judge's furious, quick-paced, jargon-laced set of instructions.

For instance, if I do not understand what differentiates murder from manslaughter in Massachusetts, I am unlikely to suddenly understand it because a judge instructs that murder requires malice and that malice does not require any ill-will toward the victim but includes a deliberate purpose to injure without legal excuse or palliation....

In a Philadelphia racketeering trial in 1993, several jurors said that they did not believe the defendant guilty but voted to convict because they mistakenly thought a hung jury was unacceptable.

Legal realist critics have pointed out since the beginning of the century that modern jury procedures mask a charade: we have judges go through the motions of instructing jurors on the law and tell them they must abide by the instructions, but we suspect that jurors do not fathom the instructions and fall back on their own gut reactions or common sense in deciding how the case should come out. To anyone who has ever witnessed a judge instructing a jury, it is clear that our system does not even pretend that the instructions are meaningful. Rarely are jurors even provided with written copies of the instructions; little attempt is made to translate jargon into common language. Most annoying of all, juror questions about the instructions are usually rebuffed with verbatim rereadings of the same instructions.

The second difficulty, as our predecessors appreciated, is that the world outside the courtroom does not neatly divide questions of fact from questions of law. When we ask jurors to decide, as a matter of fact, whether the defendant acted with malice, we are asking them to make a complicated assessment of the nature of the defendant's mental state—an inquiry far different from finding facts in the who did what, when, and where sense. To label the defendant's behavior malicious is partly to find the historical facts, but it is also to render a judgment about its blameworthiness. Juries are constantly presented with these mixed questions that jump the artificial law/fact boundary. This is true in negligence cases, where juries decide the fact of whether a defendant's behavior fell below the behavior expected of a reasonable person. It is true in obscenity cases, where juries apply "contemporary community standards" to decide the fact of whether the work in question is pornographic. So here too, against official theory, we have to admit that juries do what we say they are not equipped to do: they decide what the law means by "negligence" or "obscenity" or even "murder."

The practical impossibility of abiding by the fact/law distinction casts a new light on the earnest attempts of American law to stamp out the tradition of jury nullification. History teaches us that jurors escape from all kinds of legal straitjackets designed to restrain conscientious acquittals in criminal trials.

And this is the way it ought to be. Many of the arguments that the Supreme Court laid down in *Sparf* stripping juries of any right to decide legal questions, have no relevance to what jury nullification is about—the right to set aside the law only to acquit, never to convict. As a doctrine, jury nullification poses no threat to the accused; it is in fact the time-honored way of permitting juries to leaven the law with leniency.

To permit juries to show mercy by not enforcing the law in a given case is hardly to destroy the fabric of a society under law. Indeed, putting pressure on jurors to convict against their conscience would seem to threaten the integrity of the law far more seriously. Our current system, in which we tell jurors they must apply the law in every case no matter how unjust the results seem to them, opens the chasm between law and popular beliefs that the jury system exists to prevent.

This is not to deny that jury nullification sometimes goes badly. Even if limited to acquittals against the law, it gives us the Emmett Till jury along with the William Penn jury. There is no denying, as the Supreme Court said in another context, that "the power to be lenient is the power to discriminate." It is for this reason that the Massachusetts affiliate of the American Civil Liberties Union (ACLU) took a firm stance against a bill, introduced in the state legislature in 1991, that would have amended the jury trial handbook to inform jurors that they could acquit "according to their conscience" if they felt "the law as charged by the judge is unjust or wrongly applied to the defendant(s)." The ACLU chapter believed that "jurors often manage to control their own strong prejudices because the judge tells them they must." Its fear was that jury nullification would be an open invitation for jurors to unleash their prejudices in the name of conscience.

The ACLU affiliate's stance against jury nullification is a succinct expression of the collapsed faith in the virtue of jurors that drives the declining role of jurors at trial. In that group's judgment, jury nullification encourages jurors not to rise above the law to consult fundamental justice but to fall below law into brute bias. One is left to wonder whether the rejection of jury nullification is not a rejection of the idea of the jury altogether.

Suppose we were to inform jurors that nullification is an

option. Is the Massachusetts chapter of the ACLU right to fear dire consequences—a sudden bursting of prejudice through legal dikes? In the two states that do instruct about nullification—Indiana and Maryland—judges have not detected any dramatic rise in the frequency of nullification. Alan Scheflin and Jon Van Dyke, the leading scholars of jury nullification, reported recently on an empirical study where the effect of jury nullification instructions on mock jurors depended on the issue involved. Juries given nullification instructions were not more likely to acquit a college student charged with driving drunk and killing a pedestrian; in fact, they were less likely to acquit than juries given standard instructions. On the other hand, receiving a nullification instruction did increase the number of mock juries that acquitted a nurse charged with the mercy killing of a terminally ill cancer patient. It is encouraging that nullification instructions left the mock jurors able to distinguish the merits of pardoning the nurse and not acquitting the drunk driver....

Either openly displayed or hidden, nullification remains a timeless strategy for jurors seeking to bring law into line with their conscience. This reconciliation is what the jury system is about, for better or worse. Official disapproval of jury nullification may drive it underground, seeking disguise in fact-finding,...but, as long as we have juries, we will have nullification and verdicts according to conscience. Some of those verdicts will outrage us, others will inspire us. But always nullification will give us the full drama of democracy, as citizen-jurors assume on our behalf the task of deliberating about law in relation to justice.

Racially Based Jury Nullification:
Black Power in the Criminal Justice System?

The Prisoners Self Help Legal Clinic. From *The Bridge: Self-Help Legal News,*
October 1996, Editorial Commentary on an essay by Paul Butler, Esq.,
105 *Yale Law Journal* 677 (December 1995).

Introduction

"What is logical to the oppressor isn't logical to the oppressed. And what is reason to the oppressor isn't reason to the oppressed...There just has to be a new system of reason and logic devised by us who are at the bottom, if we want to get some results in this struggle that is called 'the Negro revolution.'" Paul Butler, a former Special Assistant U.S. Attorney, now Associate Professor of Law at George Washington University Law School, begins his article on jury nullification with this quote from Malcolm X.

A juror is said to have engaged in jury nullification if, although persuaded that the accused did take the actions which are alleged, she votes to acquit. Butler describes how lawyers and judges throughout the U.S. are increasingly aware that some African-American jurors, reflecting a desire not to send another black man to jail, vote to acquit black defendants whom they may think are guilty of the crime for which they have been charged. In an effort to frame this spontaneous response within the American tradition of jury nullification, Butler argues that the race of a black defendant can be a morally appropriated factor for jurors to consciously consider in reaching a verdict of not guilty.

In his essay, Butler argues that the failure of the law to confront the impact of race in the United States provides an opening for unauthorized responses by jurors...that black jurors should actively recognize their potential for 'deciding justice.'...

Objections to Nullification

Objections to jury nullification take two forms: principled objections to weakening the "rule of law," and practical objections that the practice will hurt more black people than it helps. Butler replies that the rule of law has worked to the disadvantage of people of African descent, and is an unreliable safeguard, and that whites regularly use jury nullification to support their own interests....

Butler contends that when white jurors apply nullification to cases with white defendants, "then they, like the black jurors, would be choosing to opt out of the criminal justice system." That would be "excellent," because it would then focus attention on alternative methods of correcting antisocial conduct much sooner than if only African-Americans raised the issue. Historically, however, it is far from clear that jury independence by white jurors was neutral in its effect on members of the black community. Nor is it certain that the advantages gained by the release of some black defendants can offset the risk to the black community of "opting out" of the criminal justice system....

Moral Arguments for Nullification

Butler sees moral justification for more than one kind of juror nullification. He clearly affirms the traditional vote to nullify a law which is wrong, or a law that has been wrongly applied. Where Butler breaks new ground is in his argument that jurors who believe in the value of a law and believe that the defendant broke the law can still vote to acquit based upon a refusal to agree with the probable punishment....[That] the African-American community should use the power they now have to create change....

Prison and Community Safety

Butler argues that criminal law enforcement benefits African-Americans "when locking up black men means that violent criminals who attack those most vulnerable are off the streets."...

Butler believes that the criminal law is unjust when it uses punishment to treat social problems that are the result of racism and that should be addressed by other means, such as medical care (for drug addiction) or the redistribution of wealth. His conclusion is: "If the criminal law is unjust, there is no duty to support it." It isn't clear from Butler's discussion how his distinction between violent and non-violent offenders fits with his evaluation of the law as unjust. Mandatory minimum sentences might prompt a juror to question whether even a violent crime warrants a 25-50 year sentence....

If Butler's model is followed, "the result would be that fewer black people would go to prison," yet the community would be protected against harmful conduct. His justification for incarceration is deterrence and isolation. Therefore, he assumes (not totally justifiably) that regardless of the reasons for their antisocial conduct, people who are violent should be separated from the community for the sake of the nonviolent. But with the nonviolent criminal, "as long as (that) person will not hurt anyone, the community needs him there to help." As for rehabilitation, the traditional justification for punishment, Butler understands that it is no longer an objective of U.S. criminal law, and if anything, prison has an anti-rehabilitative effect.

Under his proposal, the black community would not simply leave the lawbreaker be; it would encourage his education and provide his health care (including drug treatment) and, if necessary, sue him for child support. It would also include community protection against antisocial conduct, such as community security patrols. In other words, Butler's proposal is for responsible self-help by the black community outside the criminal courtroom as well as inside it....

The Activist Juror

In choosing to acquit, the black juror engages in an act of lawful civil disobedience. She is choosing not to be the only color-blind actor in the criminal process. While this might seem contrary to the U.S. ideal of equality under the law, according to Butler, that ideal never applied to African-Americans.

Butler urges every African-American to ask herself whether the operation of the criminal law in the U.S. advances the interests of black people. And "if it does not, the doctrine of jury nullification affords African-American jurors the opportunity to control the authority of the law over some African-American criminal defendants." In essence, it enables black people to "opt out" of the U.S. criminal law.

While Butler's proposal makes the argument for racially based jury nullification, he also sees that reasonable doubt—the other legal justification for acquittal—may be racially based as well: "What is reasonable to an African-American may not be reasonable to a white person."...

Realizing that prosecutors would probably try to identify and excuse jurors likely to nullify through voir dire (questioning of potential jurors), Butler sees that the African-American juror would then be placed in the difficult position of having to choose between revealing her racial sympathy, and thus surrendering her power, or denying her racial sympathy, and thus committing perjury. Butler then reaches a conclusion that is truly remarkable for a former U.S. attorney: "(T)he legal and moral case for jury nullification might lead the juror to believe that her perjury would be morally justifiable." To clarify the issue of whether a lie under oath is ever justifiable, Butler ponders what his own reaction would be if he were being considered for a jury that had the power to sentence a defendant to death.

Knowing that the Supreme Court has ruled that people opposed to the death penalty may be challenged by the prosecution from sitting as jurors in capital cases (see Witherspoon v. Illinois), and believing that capital punishment is morally wrong, Butler "would have no compunction about lying about this belief during voir dire if my lie could prevent the government from killing a human being!"

While Butler hopes that all black jurors will follow his proposal, he notes that even if only a few choose nullification, it could have significant impact because in most U.S. jurisdictions...jury verdicts in criminal cases must be unanimous. One juror could prevent the conviction of a defendant. The prosecutor would then have to retry the case "and risk facing another African-American juror with emancipation tendencies." Butler hopes that "there are enough of us out there, fed up with prison as the answer to black desperation and white supremacy, to cause retrial after retrial, until finally the United States 'retries' its idea of justice."

From the PSHLC

Nothing in this discussion should imply that a morally self-conscious jury who acquits a guilty person is "nullifying" the guilt. It is only the injustice of the procedure and/or penalty which have been nullified. The question of degrees of culpability and potential alternative community-based punishments are recognized, but not developed, in Butler's essay. It is essential that the discussion of jury independence not be confused with a denial of the blameworthiness, or culpability, of those who do harm to others.

At the Prisoners Self Help Legal Clinic, there is active support for the general issue of self-conscious jury independence, and differing levels of agreement with the arguments made by Paul Butler. In particular, members of the Clinic have disagreed about whether race is in fact the crucial factor in deciding to reject a prison sentence through nullification, about which kinds of criminals can be justifiably spared the penalty of imprisonment, and about whether the African-American community will be best served by the course of action which Paul Butler recommends.

Reprinted from *The Bridge,* with the permission of the members of the Prisoners Self Help Legal Clinic, 2 Washington Place, Newark, NJ 07102.

EIGHT

How to
Improve Juries

They wanted a chance to go before a jury, and let that jury
fairly decide. They would have been better off if they could
have abandoned all the legal processes and lawyers' games and
been allowed just to stand up and tell their story.

—Barbara Kingsolver, *Holding the Line: Women in the*
Great Arizona Mine Strike of 1983, (ILR Press, 1989)

❧   ❧   ❧

ONLY ONE JUROR on the Aguirre jury was a hold-out, for a while, in an 11-to-1 vote. That vote came on the third defendant we voted on, five weeks into deliberations.

We had agreed to start voting on those defendants who had the fewest charges and the least evidence against them. The first one was Ruben, a disabled and apparently alcoholic brother-in-law of the alleged ringleader, Gabe. We went around the table and everyone easily said "not guilty" to his being a member of a conspiracy to distribute more than 1,000 kilograms of marijuana.

The second vote concerned Michael, Gabe's son, who had once been arrested and placed on probation for having packages of marijuana wrapped as presents in the trunk of the car he was driving. (We had been shown pictures of those packages.) On going around the table again he too was easily found "not guilty" of the conspiracy.

The third vote was about Saul, a defendant connected to the Aguirre family only as an employee and temporary ranch hand. There were two charges against him: distributing more than 100 kilos of marijuana together with Gabe and belonging to the "conspiracy." As we went around the table on the distribution charge, yet again the vote was easily "not guilty." It was when we got to the conspiracy charge that our unanimity faltered. The factual question was if and to what extent he had once helped to load marijuana onto a truck. On the first go-around, five people were "unsure." Later that day, four of them changed their votes to "not guilty." It was only a couple of weeks later that the single hold-out vote was quietly changed to "not guilty," by the juror leaning over and whispering to the foreperson.

That meant that three defendants were acquitted, on a total of four counts.

After the consideration of that third defendant, the serious jury splits began and continued for the next month, until we accepted the reality that we were not going to change our votes. We were deadlocked on six defendants, with a total of 27 counts against them. Fourteen were counts against the alleged ringleader; he was found "not guilty" on one, a money laundering charge of buying a house with his sister Paula and her husband, although his name was not on any of the associated papers.

The number of counts/charges the jury was deadlocked on totaled 26. Twelve votes of the deadlocked 26 were almost evenly split. Fewer than half, or 13 of the original 31 charges, had a discernible majority for conviction. The final votes were:

Number of Charges	Guilty	Not Guilty
2	5	7
8	6	6
2	8	4
11	9	3
1	4	8
2	7	5

Of the jurors, 4 voted guilty on all 26 deadlocked votes, 1 voted guilty on 23 deadlocked votes, 1 voted guilty on 21 deadlocked votes, 2 voted guilty on 16 deadlocked votes, 1 voted guilty on 11 deadlocked votes, and 3 always voted "not guilty."

Two jurors who were friends from work sat next to each other during deliberations and voted the same way. The two Navajo women, who did not sit next to each other, voted differently only three times. The three Anglos voted differently from each other, as did the seven Hispanics.

I was not in complete agreement with the final decisions of the jury; no one was. It was our diversity that led to our lack of agreement. Since we were a good cross-section of the community, even though we could not resolve our conflicting opinions, our decisions were an accurate reflection of the opinions of the community as a whole concerning the issues of this trial. That made our decisions appropriate. It reinforces my belief that diversity on juries is essential to good decisions. If juries are indeed to be the conscience of the community, as I believe is proper, they must represent the full range of community opinion, experience, lifestyle, points of view and values, be they held by many people or few.

In general, the jurors appeared very anxious to do what they understood they were supposed to do: to follow the judge's directions.

If more of the jurors had known or believed that it was proper for them to vote their consciences, the result could only have been more acquittals in this case.

Since juries are so controversial, one too frequently mentioned method of improving them has been to suggest that they be eliminated, or at least severely cut back. Juries, however, are an essential democratic institution when they represent their communities and require unanimous verdicts. The following readings reflect this point of view.

A Jury System for Jurors

Editorial, *The New York Times,* October 27, 1994.

IT IS NO SECRET that the jury selection system in New York is a disgrace. For years it has operated mainly for the convenience of lawyers, judges and court personnel, in roughly that order.

For jurors—that is to say, the ordinary citizens summoned to decide cases and dispense justice—it has been a monumental inconvenience. A special commission appointed by Chief Judge Judith Kaye now recommends comprehensive jury reform.

One word comes to mind: Hallelujah.

Judge Kaye's reform package calls for new rules and new laws to address nearly every disgraceful feature of the system. Clean up the jury rooms. Raise the daily pay of $15 to something comparable to the $40 for Federal jury service. Cut down on the arbitrary challenges the lawyers use to bump qualified jurors. Let each juror off after serving one day or one trial (that would not happen right away in New York City, where the caseload is unusually heavy).

Further, and perhaps most important in terms of equity, the commission says that all citizens should share the privilege and burden of jury duty. To that end, it recommends abolishing two dozen professional exemptions and reaching out for a true community cross-section.

In the course of its research, the commission got to the bottom of why some New Yorkers are summoned every other year while others are never touched. The main culprits are sloppy record-keeping and excessive reliance on voter registration, driver license and tax lists. Not surprisingly, the practice of drawing jurors from those three lists has discriminated against minorities and those with low incomes.

Lawyers have long had a lock on civil jury selection under procedures unique to New York. In those cases the lawyers pick jurors without the judge even being in the room. They make their own rules, keep their own hours and often act as though the potential jurors' time had no value. A citizen may well ask what the judges are doing that is more important than presiding over the selection of juries. Judge Kaye prudently calls for pilot projects in several districts that surely will show the superiority of having judges preside.

New York law also requires sequestering, feeding and housing jurors in all criminal cases once deliberations begin. But is that necessary in all cases?

A few sensational cases require that extra hardship, but under present procedures New York judges are not trusted to decide which ones qualify. The expense, $4 million a year, is intolerable in a state struggling to maintain vital services. Nevertheless, the court officers' union, clinging to valued overtime pay, has for years defeated legislative efforts to change the system. Judge Kaye rightly recommends trying again to shame the Legislature into giving judges the discretion they have in every other state.

Judge Kaye promises to make the changes that are within her control and lobby Albany for others. Decent juror pay, reducing the arbitrary challenges, eliminating the unfair exemptions and giving judges control over sequestering all need approval by the Legislature.

The commission, headed by Colleen McMahon of the New York bar, has made a persuasive case for Albany's respectful attention. Like many New Yorkers, the Legislature has been too content for too long with an abusive system that can only breed cynicism in those who are asked to serve it.

❧ ❧ ❧

Power to the Jury: A Bill of Rights for Jurors

by Mary Timothy. From *Jury Woman* (Glide Publications, 1974).

THE JURY—a collection of twelve human beings or the concept of the fulcrum of justice—is not fragile. But it is susceptible to manipulation and coercion by powers and circumstances.

Some undermining of the power of the jury is the result of self-protective measures by the prosecutors, defenders and judges as they strive to improve and perpetuate their order; some results merely from changing circumstances as the population and economy of an area shift. Undermining may be done knowingly and unknowingly. But whatever the source or intention, the possibility and actuality of obstruction must inevitably affect justice.

Why has the situation remained unvoiced and unchanged?

The jury system has no vested interest defenders. Because of the transitory role of jurors, they have not become a socio-economic group, have not expressed their needs, have not delineated or exercised their rights.

The jury system has no experts. Only someone who has served on a jury can fully appreciate the problems involved and the very nature of the selection process precludes anyone from serving frequently enough to become aware of the extent of these problems.

The judiciary—the lawyers, judges, court officials—look on jurors as tools to facilitate the purposes of the court (that is, themselves).

Alienated members of our society equate the jury system with the rest of the judicial system, in which they place little trust.

The general citizenry seldom anticipates any personal need for protection by the jury system since they feel no threat of ever being falsely accused of a crime; therefore they consider jury duty an unpleasant obligation, an interruption of their daily lives, something to be avoided.

Yet we who have served on juries have found our service to be an experience which often makes us become strong defenders of this system of jurisprudence which allows a citizen to sit in judgment.

From our unique perspective, we also become its greatest critics, aware that the rights of all jurors can be reduced to a single simple right and need—*the right to insist on an atmosphere in which a person can make a reasoned judgment.* I have the following suggestions which could strengthen the jury system.

1. *Jurors have a right to adequate financial remuneration.* Five dollars a day...is nothing but token payment, and as a token it is insulting....

2. *Jurors should be fully informed of the "rules of the game" before the trial commences.* We should be informed of our rights to take notes, to ask questions, to insist on clarification of issues.

In the [Angela] Davis trial none of us knew or were informed whether we would be allowed to take notes. Some of us tried it; nothing happened. We were not frowned on by the judge. He didn't send his bailiff over to the jury box to snatch the notebooks from our hands. So we decided that notetaking must be all right.

One of the Davis jurors asked for clarification on a bit of evidence. He merely raised his hand and asked, "I don't understand—is that the North Arch, or the South Arch?" (The Marin County Courthouse had two arches.) Judge Arnason abruptly announced that he would not receive questions directly from the jury. If we had any questions we were to write them on a piece of paper and hand it to the bailiff, who would then relay it to the judge, who would read the question to himself and make a decision as to whether or not to allow the question to be asked.

So...we decided not to bother with questions. Jurors should have specific instruction as to what actions on our part could lead to dismissal from the jury or cause a mistrial. No doubt must remain in a juror's mind as to what the limits on personal behavior are.

In 1975, in a San Francisco federal court, the presiding judge expelled two women from the jury after a special agent of the Internal Revenue Service testified that he had been sitting next to them at lunch that day when they had "discussed" the case. One woman was quoted as having said that she felt sorry for one of the defense witnesses, "… he's seen better days." The other woman just nodded her head. For this exchange, which they admitted could have taken place, they were fined $25 for contempt of court and their names were ordered removed forever from the federal jury rolls.

True, jurors are routinely instructed that they should not discuss the case with anyone, not even with their fellow jurors until deliberations begin. But the phrase "discuss the case" means different things to different people. What it means to the court should be strictly defined to the jurors and the punishment for not strictly obeying the ruling should be delineated.

U.S. District Judge Luther Youngdahl, the same judge who expelled the two women, at the completion of that trial ordered the jury not to discuss the case with anyone. Apparently no one wishes to challenge such arbitrary rulings by judges in their dealings with jurors. Once the case is over no further interest remains in protecting the jurors' rights to freedom of speech. May a judge impose such restrictions on a jury? Such actions, if left unchallenged by disinterested attorneys and unorganized jurors, will erode the remaining rights of the jury member.

At the present time, the instructions received by jurors are frequently haphazard, varying from county to county and state to state, and are always presented to them by judges or jury commissioners. Jury handbooks, instruction manuals, even published reference books available to the public become a further means of projecting the judicial identity through the jury.

Therefore, a commission of former jurors should prepare a comprehensive handbook which would delineate the rights of the juror as well as their duties.

3. Jurors have the right to make individual, independent judgments.

A sense of identification with the judge seems to be almost universal among jurors. Uncertain and accustomed to conforming, we accept what is told us by authorities and we are even grateful for the instruction. Suddenly made aware of our own inadequacies, our lack of knowledge and competence, we follow the judge's instructions closely; by reflecting his attitudes and reactions we become more secure in our new role.

For example, a juror has been quoted as saying, "... but the way the judge charged us, there was no choice." *(The Trial of Dr. Spock,* by Jessica Mitford, New York: Alfred A. Knopf, Inc., 1969).

Jurors have the duty to ignore any prejudicial statements, rulings or attitudes of the judge. Judges are seldom chosen from the minority peoples, they are seldom women, they are almost always firmly aligned with one of the two major political parties—and they are never young.

Even when a judge conducts a trial faultlessly, his influence on an unsophisticated juror may lead to perversion of the purposes of the jury system. The jury so influenced becomes an extension of the court rather than an extension of the community it represents.

An often-cited example of a jury acting as an extension of their community occurred in Seattle, Washington, in December, 1972. A group of anti-war activists were charged with attempting to halt a munitions train. They readily admitted that they had indeed made such an attempt. Despite this admission the jury acquitted them; even though they had broken the law, they were not guilty in the judgment of the jury.

No absolute set of rules fits all cases. Therefore the wording of the law is replete with phrases such as reasonable doubt, ordinary reasonable man, reasonable time.... "Reasonableness" is best defined by community standards, not by the value judgments of one man.

The right, in fact the duty, of the jury to interpret the law in light of the standards of our changing world is seldom if ever made clear to jurors. We are told over and over that we are serving on the jury merely to judge facts. In truth jurors are presented with a series of "facts" as evidence and then given the choice of many conclusions. Seldom is a clear-cut single answer to be drawn from the evidence. It is the value placed on the evidence that allows the jury to reach a decision. The value evolves from community standards and is best represented by a cross section of people with various experiences and knowledge.

4. *Jurors have the right to serve on juries which include people from varied socioeconomic groups....*The residual group from which the selection of jurors is made becomes very homogeneous. This arbitrary exclusion of various groups lessens the representation of the community.

5. *Jurors have a right to have members of minorities included on the jury.*

The common conception is that having minorities on juries is of interest only to a minority defendant. But it is critically important to members of the jury that their group be as heterogeneous as possible in order to add insight and awareness to the problems of judging another human being.

An all-white, middle-class, middle-income jury whose members are employed by the large industries in an area is placed in a difficult position when trying to deal with evidence relating to mores and behavior standards of many of those accused of crimes....

The civil rights of those called for jury duty must be protected. The selection process must be conducted in a manner comparable to the affirmative action programs in other areas of our lives during the past few years. Preferential selection of minorities to jury lists must be practiced until it becomes impossible for them to be prevented from serving.

6. *Jurors have a right not to be stereotyped.* Even as the defendant should not be judged because of her or his race, religion, dress, or the like, neither should the prospective juror be thus judged. Being eliminated from the jury by either the judge or one of the attorneys is insulting. One feels somehow demeaned when an individual who

knows nothing about you decides that you cannot be a fair unprejudiced person.

For the one being questioned, to reveal one's individuality in court is most difficult. It is frightening to sit in a jury box, the center of attention, while you are being asked about your background, your beliefs, your ability to be fair; most people are concerned with making this public and recorded presentation of themselves as "normal" as possible. In many cases the questioning is done by the judge. No matter what your prejudices, when His Honor the Judge says, "Now M– 'X,' you will be able to judge the defendant fairly, won't you?" the answer is most likely to be, "Yes, Your Honor!"...

7. Jurors have a right to privacy....The juror is not on trial.

8. Jurors have a right to be free from threats, both direct and implied. The laws are explicit in protecting people from direct threats. Jury tampering is a serious offense. However, pressures can be exerted in many subtle ways.

When the police, with the concurrence of the judge, build eight-foot-high cyclone security fences, place armed guards at every entrance to the building, conduct body searches of everyone entering the area (even the jurors themselves), they are displaying the awesome power of law enforcement. While ostensibly done for the protection of the jurors, among others, such security measures create an atmosphere of fear and oppression the effect of which is impossible to measure.

When the defendant or defendants are brought into the courtroom handcuffed, shackled and chained to chairs bolted to the floor, the jury is being told that they should be tremendously afraid of that defendant. When a witness is chained to the witness stand and additional armed deputies are stationed around the courtroom, the jury is again being told they should be afraid. How then can a juror accept the testimony of this witness with the same objectivity as that of other witnesses?

A threat need not relate to physical violence; it can also relate to psychological influences. Thus the sequestering of juries throughout a trial is another example of an implied threat. In my opinion, this action is a very real and direct assault on the jury system. It quickly eliminates many people from the jury—those who will not allow themselves to be so manipulated. It makes a prisoner of the juror.

9. *Jurors have a right to be free from investigation.* In the Angela Davis trial, the panel of veniremen was investigated very thoroughly outside the court as well as during the extensive public voir dire questioning in court.

It was readily apparent that the prosecution had available all records of government agencies such as police, courts, Alcoholic Beverage Commission, welfare and relief agencies, and the like. The defense used volunteer investigators who checked the neighborhoods in which we lived, the attitudes of our neighbors and fellow employees toward us. Psychologists advised the attorneys. Even a handwriting expert was used to analyze our suitability to serve....

The government, losing so many of these politically important cases, will blame the juries rather than acknowledge the inadequacy of its own cases and so will be forced to expand the already formidable investigations of prospective jurors....In addition to the obvious and awful consequences, such erosions of our jury system and encroachments of our liberties would result in the jury becoming merely an extension of the court, instead of a citizen jury that can stand between the accused and the accuser.

Our implementation of justice is on trial now, and we are the jurors—those who have served in the jury boxes and in the jails, those yet to be called and yet to be accused, those who never expect to become involved. Deliberation is needed. We must bring in a verdict.

Power to the jury.

❧ ❧ ❧

Juries on Trial

by Jeffrey Toobin, *The New Yorker,* October 31, 1994.

...WITH A SINGLE STEP...the jury system could save time and money, reduce racial and gender bias, enhance its efficiency, and add to the public perception that it yields fair results: all it would take is the elimination of peremptory challenges....

When Americans discuss jury selection, what they are really talking about, for the most part, is the exercise of peremptory challenges. In most jurisdictions, prospective jurors are assembled randomly from voter registration or driver's-license lists. After voir dire, both sides are allowed to ask the judge to remove any number of jurors "for cause"; that is, because of an identifiable bias rendering them unfit to serve. In most cases, though, successful for-cause challenges are rare; few jurors are so obviously prejudiced that judges feel compelled to exclude them. The real grist of jury selection comes in the exercise of preremptories. "Unlike challenges for cause, peremptory strikes require no justification, no spoken word of explanation, no reason at all beyond a hunch, an intuition."...For lawyers with rich clients, however, making the hunches more scientific has become a major industry.

...Trial lawyers do nothing but eliminate potential jurors on the basis of group biases. Abolishing preremptories would deprive lawyers of that opportunity....

If lawyers were limited to for-cause challenges, jury selection would rarely take more than a couple of hours....A jury system without peremptory challenges would better reflect the ideal of impartial justice rendered from a true cross-section of the community.

Reprinted with permission of the author.
Jeffrey Toobin is a staff writer at *The New Yorker* and legal analyst for ABC News.

Conclusion

Who we listen to determines what we hear. Where we stand determines what we see. What we do determines who we are.

—Robert McAfee Brown

🌿　🌿　🌿

THE AGUIRRE CASE was very much affected by the existence of a border between the United States and Mexico that is highly regulated vis-a-vis Mexican nationals. Like prisons, our closed southern border has racist effects. Living in the southwestern part of the country makes this highly visible. Mexico and New Mexico have, after all, only been different countries for 150 years. As a bumper sticker I once saw said, "We didn't cross the border, the border crossed us."

At the trial, even crossing the border was presented as suspect. A lot of evidence had to do with people and goods—ore, cattle, marijuana and money—coming into the United States from Mexico. The prosecution always depicted this as shady. The prosecutors also acted very annoyed that they could not subpoena witnesses or bank records from Mexico—as if somehow Mexico's being a separate country were part of a deliberate attempt to conceal information.

The prosecution chronicled here resulted in six people being imprisoned. Those six defendants were sent to federal prisons in Arizona, California, Colorado and Texas. They have all appealed, a process that is likely, at least for some of them, to go on for years. There is no way to know how many years of prison time these six people, who the original jury never found guilty, will actually end up doing.

During my spring vacation from school the year after I had been a juror, I drove with my friend Pat from El Paso, on the border with Mexico in far west Texas—just south of New Mexico—to Brownsville, in far east Texas, 20 miles from the Gulf of Mexico. I learned a lot on that trip.

Pat met me when I arrived in El Paso and took me to supper at the house of some friends, originally from Mexico, in south El Paso. Pat, a writer, was familiar with the area because of her interest in rivers, particularly the Rio Grande, and the people who live along them.

Walking into the Guzmans' kitchen was an enormous shock for me. Three members of this family—the mother, the son and the daughter— had been character witnesses for one of the defendants when I had been a juror. They didn't recognize me, but I felt I knew them—they had spoken with such feeling and detail about their friend, who was in peril of getting as much as a 20-year sentence for conspiracy and money laundering. This defendant had been the office manager in their family plumbing business and in the process had become like another daughter in the family. After all the explanations and expressions of surprise and wonder, the daughter of the house phoned her friend, the former defendant, to share the news of the coincidence. After we had eaten, we watched the video of the daughter's recent wedding, in which her friend the defendant had been a bridesmaid.

When the Guzmans had moved across the river from Juarez to El Paso, they had very little. They used to salvage sheet metal from the dump, flatten it by running back and forth over it with their old pick up and resell it at local flea markets. Now the son and daughter are both teachers in the El Paso public schools.

As I was coming back from my trip, on the bus from San Antonio to El Paso, agents from the Border Patrol got on the bus and walked up and down the aisle looking at people. A young teenager across the aisle flashed her mother an anguished look. We were a busload of a variety of people. Who would turn out to be "us" and who "them"?

THE PROFESSIONALS WHO DOMINATE TRIALS often don't like or respect juries. It is true they can't completely control them. The jury is the entity in the courtroom that is the most like the defendants, and is supposed to be, a "jury of your peers." One of the important ways juries have value for society is that they look at things differently than the experts do, and therefore provide a check on them. It is exactly their different point of view and independence that is valuable to the common good. Jurors cannot avoid using what they know from outside of the courtroom, where true justice lies.

In a democracy, in theory, we hire the experts to serve us, not vice versa. Yet the opposite is what often happens. How many of us feel at the mercy of our physicians, rather than as if we have hired them? We find them arrogant, intimidating and uninformative, not to mention that they keep us waiting a long time.

The common people are the best judge of the common good. According to *Judging the Jury*, "When the evidence was clear, the jury was inclined to follow the law, but when it was unclear, jurors felt liberated to give rein to their own sense of justice and equity."

Laws and how they are applied should be helpful to the community as a whole. That is, they should not be classist, or homophobic, or sexist or racist. But since society can be classist, homophobic, sexist and racist, the effects of the laws can be too. Each of us must take responsibility to minimize these bad effects.

The experience of being a juror raised many questions in my mind. One of the most important is: Why does the United States rely so heavily on punishment to create positive change? We appear to be one of the very few countries to do so.

My students were surprised at the idea that an individual, even a teacher, could do something in the real world that would directly affect others' lives, such as, for example, those of the defendants in a trial. The students appeared impressed with this idea, but needed to think about its implications. Such action gave the word "responsibility" a whole new dimension.

The positive part of serving as a juror was having the opportunity as well as the obligation to act in the public arena according to one's conscience.

The concluding readings sum up the themes of personal responsibility, positive resolution of disagreements and how we can inspire each other to do our best for ourselves and our communities.

❦ ❦ ❦

The Need to Support, Monitor, and Discipline Police

by Rev. Virginia Mackey, *Justicia,* October 1994.

Support? Yes, helping the community to determine the legitimate police function and support those police who are accountable to it. The community expects a lot: the more interaction there is with the community, the less tendency for enforcement personnel to become a law unto themselves.

Monitor? Yes, because the abuses of police power have such damaging and cynical effects. There is a role for the community in monitoring accountability and helping to improve policies and procedures.

Discipline? Yes, because the goal is to change behavior, to cause police to be responsible for their actions and those of their colleagues.

There is a dramatic difference in the roots of the words discipline and punishment. In a discipline mode, the person is expected to be a "disciple," one who learns or is trained. In the punishment mode, we inflict pain on a person.

From a practical standpoint, punishment is proving futile and enormously costly in our nation's prisons. From a psychological perspective, we may perceive that the infliction of pain makes us feel "in charge" but has little to do with the need of the punished to take responsibility to change values and behavior.

From a theological perspective, the stories of a punitive God are simply that—stories that try to convey that our God wants us to be aware of the consequences of our actions. Do they increase pain and violence or foster peace and justice?

Instead of getting tough, let's get real with—*support, monitoring, discipline.*

Justicia is the Newsletter of Judicial Process Commission, Inc.,
Rochester, NY. Reprinted with permission.

The Judgment of Solomon

1 Kings 3, 16-28, *Christian Community Bible.*

Then two harlots came to the king and stood before him. One of the two women said, "Oh, my lord, this woman and I live in the same house, and I gave birth to a child while she was there with me. Three days after my child was born, this woman also gave birth. We were alone, and there was no one in the house but the two of us. Then this woman's son died during the night because she lay on him. So during the night, she got up, took my son from my side while I slept, laid it beside her and her dead son beside me. When I got up in the morning to nurse my child, I saw it was dead. But when I looked at it closely in the morning, I saw that it was not my child." The other woman said, "No, the living child is mine; the dead child is yours." To this, the first replied, "Not so, but the dead child is yours; the living child is mine." And they quarreled this way in the king's presence. Then the king said, "One says, 'This is my son who is alive; your son is dead'; the other says: 'That is not so, your son is dead; my son is the live one.'" And the king said, "Bring me a sword." When they brought the king a sword, he gave his order, "Divide the child in two and give half to one, half to the other." Then the woman whose son was alive said to the king out of pity for her son, "Oh, my lord, give her the living child but spare its life." The other woman, however, said, "It shall be neither mine nor yours. Divide it!" Then the king spoke, "Give the living child to the first woman and spare its life. She is its mother."

When all Israel heard of the judgment which the king had given, they marveled at him, seeing that God's wisdom was in him to render justice.

Cowardice Asks the Question...

by Dr. Martin Luther King Jr.

Cowardice asks the question:
is it safe?

Expediency asks the question:
is it politic?

Vanity asks the question:
is it popular?

But conscience asks the question:
is it right?

And there comes a time when one must take a position that
is neither safe, nor politic, nor popular
—but one must take it because it's right.

Glossary

Appeal bond—money or property pledged to allow a convicted defendant to be released from custody while her or his appeal is being heard by the courts.

Bench trial—a trial in which the facts and the law are decided by a judge; there is no jury in a bench trial.

Charge—an accusation by the government of the commission of a crime or offense.

Count—a statement of a specific charge that includes the facts giving rise to the charge.

Criminal trial—a trial in which the government accuses a defendant of violating criminal laws; it may be either a bench trial or a jury trial.

Custodial witness—a person who testifies in a trial about documents or business records that she or he is responsible for keeping.

Discovery—a set of rules and procedures that govern the process by which people involved in a lawsuit try to find out information about each other's case before the trial.

Felony—a crime considered more serious than other crimes; felony convictions usually are punishable by more than a year in prison or by death, as opposed to misdemeanors, which are usually punishable by a year or less in jail.

Habeas corpus petition—a request to a court to consider the legality of a defendant's imprisonment after conviction of a crime.

Nolo contendere—literally "no contest"; unlike a guilty plea, with a plea of nolo contendere, a defendant does not admit or deny the criminal charges against her or him.

Petit jury service—service on a jury in a trial, as distinguished from grand jury service.

Rebuttal and surrebuttal—witnesses' testimony that responds to previous testimony; testimony may be followed by rebuttal testimony, which may then be followed by surrebuttal testimony.

Venireman—any person who is in a jury pool.

Voir dire—The process of jury selection. The attorneys and/or the judge question the people in the jury pool to find out what they might know about the case or any strong opinions they have about the issues in the case. The questions may be oral or in writing. The answers jury pool members give to these questions are the most important factors in jury selection.

Selected Resources

❦ ❦ ❦

Organizations

California Prison Focus—2489 Mission Street #28, San Francisco CA 94110 • (415) 452-3359. A nonprofit organization that works with and on behalf of prisoners in California's control units. Their quarterly publication is *Prison Focus*.

Centurion Ministries—James McClosky, Director, 32 Nassau Street, Princeton NJ 08542. Investigates and advocates for a limited number of wrongful conviction cases. As of April 1998, Centurion had freed 25 people from prison and benefitted a total of 49 people in 14 jurisdictions.

Coalition for Prisoners' Rights—PO Box 1911, Santa Fe NM 87504. Their monthly newsletter, *Coalition for Prisoners' Rights Newsletter,* free to prisoners and their families, discusses and analyzes prison conditions and policy. Half of each issue is devoted to excerpts from letters by those imprisoned. The Coalition maintains a variety of resource lists.

Equal Justice USA—A Project of the Quixote Center, PO Box 5206, Hyattsville MD 20782 • (301) 699-0042. The organization supports free speach for prisoners and opposes police and court corruption. Publications include *Moratorium News* and *Saga of Shame,* a book of voices against execution.

Families Against Mandatory Minimums—1612 K Street NW, Suite 1400, Washington D.C. 20006 • (202) 822-6700. Founded by prisoners' family members, their slogan is "Let the Punishment Fit the Crime." Their newsletter is *FAMM-gram*. They offer a Citizen Action Kit.

Judicial Process Commission—121 N Fitzhugh Street, Rochester NY 14614 • (716) 325-7727. Founded after the Attica prison uprising in 1971. Their newsletter is *Justicia*.

Mexican American Legal Defense & Educational Fund (MALDEF)—634 S Spring Street, 12th floor, Los Angeles CA 90014 • (213) 629-2512. Founded in 1968, its purpose is to protect the civil rights of Hispanics, including Mexican-Americans.

Murder Victims Families for Reconciliation (MVFR)—PO Box 208, Atlantic, VA 23303-0208 • (757) 824-0948. MVFR is a national organization of family members of victims of both homicide and state killings who oppose the death penalty in all cases. Its newsletter is *The Voice*.

NAACP Legal Defense and Educational Fund, Inc.—99 Hudson Street, 16th floor, New York NY 10013 • (212) 219-1900. In addition to filing habeas corpus petitions for death-sentenced prisoners, the "Inc. Fund" maintains the most complete death row-related statistics in the country.

National Criminal Justice Commission, a project of the National Center on Institutions and Alternatives (NCIA)—635 Slaters Lane, Alexandria VA 22314 • (703) 684-0373. The Commission, formed in 1994, published *The Real War on Crime* in 1996 (HarperPerennial).

National Drug Strategy Network—1899 L Street NW, Suite 500, Washington D.C. 20036 • (202) 835-9075. Publishes *NewsBriefs*, to share information about the world's drug problems and what is being done in response. The Network does not lobby and does not take positions on policy.

National Women's Law Center—11 Dupont Circle NW, Suite 800, Washington D.C. 20036 • (202) 588-5180. Published *An End to Silence: Women Prisoners Handbook on Identifying and Addressing Sexual Misconduct* in 1998.

The Sentencing Project—918 F Street NW, Washington D.C. 20004
• (202) 628-0871. A sentencing-reform advocacy group, the Project
sponsors the Campaign for an Effective Crime Policy and publishes a
series entitled "Americans Behind Bars."

Writings and Authors

Paul Butler, former federal prosecutor, currently teaching criminal
law at George Washington University Law School in Washington
D.C. Writings by him include:

- "Black Jurors: Right to Acquit?" *Harper's Magazine,* December 1995.
- "Justice in Black and White," *The Boston Sunday Globe,* November 19, 1995.

Joseph Fletcher, *Situational Ethics—the New Morality,* Westminster
Press, 1966.

G. Thomas Munsterman, Paula L. Hannaford, and G. Marc White-
head, editors, *Jury Trial Innovations,* National Center for State Courts,
1997.

Mary Timothy, *Jury Woman, The Story of the Trial of Angela Y. Davis—
written by a member of the jury,* Glide Publications/Empty Press, 1974.

Index

🌿 🌿 🌿

Abu-Jamal, Mumia, 86–87
ACLU (American Civil Liberties Union),
    143, 144
Alcohol, *see* Drugs
American Jury, The , 100, 101
American Medical Association, 83
Anaya, Toney, 84
Anslinger, Jacob, 73
Anthony, Susan B., 98
Appeals, legal, basis for, 35–36
Attorneys, 13, 34–50, 85
    and jury selection, 161
    and preremptory challenges, 162
    appellate, 36–37
    corruption of, 60
    in Aguirre trial, 2–3, 29, 32, 52–54, 85,
        94–95, 107, 163
    in Gonzalez trial, 124–125
    in Martinez trial, 85
    undermining the power of the jury,
        155

Bench trials, *see* Judges
Border, U.S.-Mexico
    and Aguirre trial, 2, 163
    and drug smuggling, 59
    See also U.S. Border Patrol
Burden of proof, 4
    See also Innocence, presumption of
Butler, Paul, 137, 145–149

Campaign Against Marijuana Planting
    (CAMP), 68
Capital punishment, *see* Death Penalty
Charges
    in Aguirre trial, 14, 32, 103
    in Gonzalez trial, 124
Chicago, University of, Jury Project, 100
Cigarettes, *see* Drugs
Civil cases, 1
Civil disobedience, 147
    See also Jury nullification
Cocaine, 18, 20, 56, 58, 59, 62, 63, 64, 67,
    74–75, 82
    and prison sentences, 20, 26–28
    in Aguirre case, 32
    health effects of, 56–57, 61, 63
    See also Drugs
Code of Judicial Conduct,
    New Mexico, 31
Congress (U.S.), 22, 25, 26–28, 83, 97
Constitution, *see* U.S. Constitution
Convictions
    numbers of drug-related, 55
    of the innocent, 34–50
Court personnel, x, 2–3, 29
    See also Attorneys, Judges, Marshals
Criminal cases, 1
    disposition of in U.S, 5
Criminogenics, 23, 57–58

Deadlock, *see* Juries
Death penalty, 84–92
  and public executions, 88–90
  and racism, 86–87
  as sacrifice, 91–92
  in Philadelphia and Manhattan, 87–88
  statistics, 86
  See also Sentencing
Declaration of Independence, 55
Defendants, 2
  in Aguirre trial, 14–15, 29–33
Deliberations, *see* Juries
Devlin, Lord, 99
Drug Enforcement Agency, 21, 65–71
Drugs, Crime and the Justice System:
  A National Report (U.S. Department
  of Justice), 55
Drugs
  addiction to, 62–63, 74
  and racism, 71–75
  effects on health, 56–57, 61, 63
  effects on quality of life, 58
  legalization of, 61, 73–74
  sentencing related to use of, 21–22,
    25–28, 51
  users of, by race, 18–19, 51, 71–72
  "War on," 18–19, 56–63, 64, 65–75
  See also Marijuana, Cocaine
du Pont, John E., 7–9
Dupont Chemical Company, 72

Evidence, 2
  and jury nullification, 139
  difficulties in accuracy of, 47–49
  in jury deliberations, 111, 115–116,
    135, 159
  in Aguirre case, 52–54, 104
Executions, *see* Death Penalty

Fact/law distinction, 142–144, 158–159
Fair and impartial, as standard of
  conduct for jurors, x
Federal Bureau of Narcotics, 73
Fugitive Slave Law, 133

Gangs
  and drugs, 62
  and prison sentences, 20

Guideline sentences, *see* Sentencing

Hashish, 79
  See also Marijuana
Hearst, William R., 72
Hemp, 72–73, 79–80
  See also Marijuana
Hung jury, *see* Juries, deadlocked

Indictment
  in Aguirre case, 14, 32, 52, 103
Informers, 15, 21–22, 75–79
  See also Witnesses
Innocence, presumption of, 4, 37
Instructions, *see* Judges, Juries

Judges, 2, 13, 34–50, 135
  and executions, 88–89
  and jurors' views, in sentencing,
    131–132
  and jury instructions, 157, 158
  and jury nullification, 133–140-141
  and jury selection, 160
  corruption of, 60
  decisions differing from juries, 6–7,
    99–101
  in Aguirre trial, 29–31, 32, 104,
    133–134
  instructions to juries, 14, 110, 141
  relation to defendant, 97, 99
  undermining the power of the jury,
    155
Juries
  and burden of proof, 4, 31, 115
  and executions, 88–89
  and loss of faith in, 143
  as more lenient than judges, 6–7,
    99–101
  changes in structure of, 102
  competence of, 99
  deadlocked, 31, 103, 112, 114, 141,
    151–152
  deliberations, 108–114, 134, 142
  factors in voting, x, 1–3, 114–116,
    127–129, 129, 130-132, 134
  instructions to, 14, 94, 104, 111, 112,
    134, 138, 140, 142, 144, 157, 158
  jury nullification, 133–149

need for independence of, 101, 165
power of, 96–99, 116
reform of selection process, in
   New York, 153–154
rules for, 156–157
selecting foreperson for, 108–109
sequestration of, 153–154, 161
suggestions for improving, 156–162
unanimity of, 98, 102, 110, 111,
   114, 151
undermining of, 155
Jurors
  characteristics of, in Aguirre trial, *ix,* 1,
    51–52, 104–106, 152
  deliberations of, in Aguirre trial,
    104–107, 133–134, 150-152
  deliberations of, in Gonzalez trial, 125,
    127–129
  fees paid, 5, 104, 153, 156
  numbers of potential jurors sum-
    moned in the U.S., 5
  participation in deliberations, 112
  rights of, 156–161
  treatment of, in Aguirre trial, 29
  treatment of, in Davis trial, 156, 157,
    159, 160, 161
  voting their conscience, *xi,* 98, 114,
    134, 135, 138, 152, 165, 168
  women as, 1, 94
Jury trials, 4
  numbers of in U.S., 4, 102
  conviction rates of, 6–7
  the right to have, 96

Lawyers, *see* Attorneys

Malcolm X, 145
Mandatory minimum sentences,
  see Sentencing
Marijuana, *x,* 56, 64
  and racism, 71–75
  dangers of use, 56, 64,74
  health effects of, 56–57, 61 63
  history of use, 79–83
  growing in U.S., 65–71, 79–83
  in Aguirre case, *ix, x,* 51–55
  laws against, 82

  medicinal use of, 80-81, 833
  See also Drugs
Marshals, of the court, 2
  in Aguirre trial, 30-31, 104
McCarthy, Senator Joseph, 73
Mexico, 2, 31, 67, 71, 79,105, 128

National Organization for the Reform of
  Marijuana Laws (NORML), 68, 69
Nullification,
  and racism, 145–149
  as right of juries, 133–149, 158–159
  definition of, 139, 140, 142
  in Aguirre trial, 152
  informing juries about, 136–140, 144
  judges and attorneys role in, 133–138
  See also Judges, Juries

Pataki, (New York) Governor George,
  24–25, 70, 88
Penalties, 3
Penn, William, 134, 143
Perjury
  by police, 38
  by potential jurors, 148
  by witnesses, 39
Physical evidence, 2
Police
  coercion of confession, 127
  community accountability, 166
  corruption of, 60
  manipulation of evidence or wit-
    nesses, 40-43
  "no-knock" search warrants, 75–79
  perjury, 38
  protection of jurors, 160
  racism, 76
  shoddy investigative work, 43–44
  unequal treatment by, 7–9
Preremptory challenge, *see* Attorneys
Prisoners,
  and drug offenses, 17
  blacks as, 17–18, 20-21
  characteristics of, in U.S., 17–18, 23
  Hispanics as, 17
  numbers of in U.S., 17
  treatment of, 9, 13

women as, 17–18
  See also Prisons, Sentencing
Prisons
  alternatives to, 23, 24, 147, 149
  and crime prevention, 23, 33
  and punishment, 166
  and rehabilitation, 147
  conditions in, 23
  federal budget for, 18
  in N.Y., 24
  population of in U.S., 17–18,
  purpose of, 9
Prosecutors, *see* Attorneys
Punishment, 3, 165, 166
Racism, *see* Drugs, Mexico, Nullification,
  Police, Sentencing
Reasonable doubt, 4, 101, 113, 158
  and jury nullification, 138, 139, 140,
    148, 158
  in Aguirre trial, 94–95

Sentencing
  and "3 Strikes" law, 130-132
  for drug offenses, 21–22, 24, 66
  guidelines, 25–28
  in Aguirre trial, 32
  jurors' views, 131–132
  mandatory minimums, 22, 25–28, 70,
    102, 147
  racial discrepancies, 18–19
Simpson, O.J., 7, 86, 98
Solomon, King, 167
"Street sweeps," and drug use, 19–20

"3 strikes" law, 130-132
Trials
  Aguirre case, *ix-x*, 1–3, 29–33
  errors in, 36
  Gonzalez case 117–129
  Twelve Angry Men, 113

U.S. Border Patrol, 62, 67, 120, 128, 164
U.S. Constitution, 46, 61, 96, 99, 102,
  136–140
U.S. Sentencing Commission, 25–28
U.S.A. Wrestling, 8–9

War on Drugs, *see* Drugs
Whittington, H. DeWayne, 116
Witnesses, 2
  character, 2, 104, 164
  corruption of, 60
  in Aguirre trial, 15–16, 107
  informant , 2, 39
  perjury by, 39

Zenger, John Peter, 98

Resources for

Keep up-to-date on new fundraising techniques and issues. Learn how to increase your income and diversify your sources of funding using proven, practical strategies, including special events, direct mail, major donor programs, membership campaigns and more.
$32/year; $58/2 years

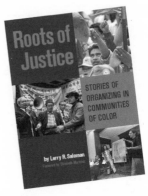

Roots of Justice recaptures some of the nearly forgotten histories of communities of color. These are the stories of people who fought back against exploitation and injustice – and won. It shows how, through organizing, ordinary people have made extraordinary contributions to change society. **$15**

Veteran organizer Gary Delgado provides a compelling look at where organizing is going and how it's changing. Called by one reviewer, "The most important analysis of community organizing since the 1960's," this book is essential reading for anyone involved in grassroots organizations. **$25**

An introduction to the most common and successful fundraising strategies in 14 of the best articles from the *Grassroots Fundraising Journal.* Small organizations can put these strategies to use immediately. This reprint collection in Spanish only. **$12**

Social Change

CHARDON PRESS...
progressive movement for social justice

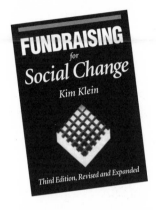

If you want to change the world, you'll want to read *Inspired Philanthropy*. No matter how much or little you have to give, you'll learn how to create a giving plan that will make your charitable giving catalytic. Through clear text and substantive exercises, you'll learn how to align your giving with your deepest values—to help bring about the very changes you want. **$25**

Kim Klein's classic how-to fundraising text teaches you everything you need to know to raise money successfully from individuals. Learn how to motivate your board of directors; analyze your constituency; plan and implement major gifts campaigns, endowments and planned giving programs; use direct mail techniques successfully; and more. **$25**

A model for linking grassroots organizing with political analysis and policy development. Using the issues of community safety and police accountability, *Justice by the People* shows how to link education with action—in 15 provocative and lively workshops. **$25**

Bulk Discounts Available!

For more information about these and many other titles, contact us for a free catalog and visit our Web site at

www.chardonpress.com

CHARDON PRESS
P.O. Box 11607, Berkeley, CA 94712
PHONE: (510) 704-8714
FAX: (510) 649-7913
E-MAIL: chardn@aol.com

CHARDON PRESS ORDER FORM

Grassroots Fundraising Journal

SUBSCRIPTIONS
Please allow 6 weeks for processing new subscriptions.

United States
- ☐ 1 year @ $32 _____
- ☐ 2 years @ $58 _____
- ☐ 3 years @ $84 _____

Canada & Overseas
- ☐ 1 year @ $39 _____
- ☐ 2 years @ $65 _____
- ☐ 3 years @ $91 _____

SUBTOTAL: $ _____

There are no tax or shipping charges for subscriptions.

REPRINT COLLECTIONS*
- ☐ The Board of Directors $10 _____
- ☐ Getting Major Gifts $10 _____
- ☐ Cómo Recaudar Fondos... $12 _____

* Please call for bulk discounts.

BACK ISSUES
- ☐ All Available Back Issues: $150 _____
- ☐ Individual Back Issues: $5 each

Single articles not available.

QUANTITY	VOLUME & NUMBER	COST

SUBTOTAL: $ _____

Books

- ☐ **Fundraising for Social Change**
  by Kim Klein
  - ____ 1–4 copies @ $25 each _____
  - ____ 5–9 copies @ $20 each _____
  - ____ 10+ copies @ $15 each _____

- ☐ **Grassroots Grants** *by Andy Robinson*
  - ____ 1–4 copies @ $25 each _____
  - ____ 5–9 copies @ $20 each _____
  - ____ 10+ copies @ $15 each _____

- ☐ **Roots of Justice** *by Larry Salomon*
  - ____ copies @ $15 each _____

- ☐ **Juries: Conscience of the Community** *by Mara Taub*
  - ____ copies @ $17 each _____

- ☐ **Justice by the People**
  by Terry Keleher/Applied Research Center
  - ____ copies @ $25 each _____

- ☐ **Beyond the Politics of Place**
  by Gary Delgado/Applied Research Center
  - ____ copies @ $25 each _____

- ☐ **Inspired Philanthropy**
  by Tracy Gary & Melissa Kohner
  - ____ copies @ $20 each _____

SUBTOTAL: $ _____

Reprints /Back Issues *Subtotal:* $ _____ +

Books *Subtotal:* $ _____ = $ _____

In CA add 8.25% sales tax to above total: $ _____

Shipping & Handling (see chart above): $ _____

SUBSCRIPTION *Subtotal:* $ _____

TOTAL AMOUNT ENCLOSED: $ _____

CREDIT CARD ORDERS
☐ MasterCard   ☐ VISA

Card #: _____

Expiration date: _____

Signature:
_____

SHIPPING/HANDLING CHARGES

ORDER TOTALLING	SHIPPING FEE
$ 5.00 – 20.00	$ 2.00
$ 20.01 – 25.00	$ 4.00
$ 25.01 – 50.00	$ 6.00
$ 50.01 – 75.00	$ 8.00
$ 75.01 – 100.00	$10.00
$100.01 or more	10% of order

☐ 2nd day air   + $5.00
☐ Overnight   + $10.00

Overseas (including Canada & Mexico):
For each shipping & handling level above,
multiply by 2 (Payment in U.S. dollars only).

Please allow 2–4 weeks for delivery.

Please make
checks payable to:
CHARDON PRESS
P.O. Box 11607
Berkeley, CA 94712

PHONE: **(510) 704-8714**

FAX: **(510) 649-7913**

E-MAIL:
chardn @aol.com

WEB PAGE:
www.chardonpress.com

Name _____

Organization _____

Address _____

City/State/Zip _____

Phone _____